Stones of Remembrance

STONES
of
REMEMBRANCE

PAT SAKS

XULON PRESS

Xulon Press
2301 Lucien Way #415
Maitland, FL 32751
407.339.4217
www.xulonpress.com

Unless otherwise indicated Scripture quotations taken from the New
King James Version (NKJV). Copyright © 1982 by Thomas Nelson,
Inc. Used by permission. All rights reserved.

Printed in the United States of America.

ISBN-13: 978-1-5456-7433-8

Dedication

And Aaron and Hur supported his hands, one on one side, and the other on the other side; and his hands were steady until the going down of the sun.
(Exodus 17:12 NKJV)

This book is dedicated to my precious friends, Lisa Piatt and Bettie Lorino, without whom it would never have happened. They were my "Aaron" and "Hur" who held up my arms whenever I got tired and discouraged and wanted to give up. I am forever grateful to God for bringing them into my life.

Acknowledgements

A number of people have helped and encouraged me on my journey writing this book. God never sends His people out alone to do His work: He always places godly companions alongside them. Jesus sent his disciples out in pairs ahead of Him to announce the kingdom of heaven was at hand.

> *After this the Lord appointed seventy-two others and sent them two by two ahead of him to every town and place where he was about to go (Luke 10:1 NIV).*

Paul was given Barnabas, Silas, and many others to support him in his mission to proclaim the resurrected Christ to the Gentiles.

> *While they were worshipping the Lord and fasting, the Holy Spirit, said, "Set apart for me Barnabas and Saul for the work to which I have called them" (Acts 13:2 NIV).*

I am no way comparing myself to these heroes of faith, but even we, in our simple journeys, are given companions chosen by God.

I need to thank the following:

My two precious friends to whom this book is dedicated, Lisa Piatt and Betty Lorino. It was through Lisa I found my "voice." She gave me the confidence to start writing and designed a beautiful website as a repository for my compositions. More importantly, she stopped me whenever

I got scared and tried to turn tail and run, which was often. Without her, this book would not have happened.

Bettie Lorino is a heaven-sent gift from God. She supported me every step of the way, taking the time to read through my scribbles and provide valuable insights. I am so grateful to God for bringing us together.

My dear friend, Tiesha Pinchinat, gave me the wise words I needed to get started. She told me not to wait for perfection because perfection would lead to paralysis. I followed her advice and a book was born.

Connie Padmore, whose *Unveiled* teaching and insights were invaluable in giving me the self-confidence and courage to continue writing, even to the point of getting up on stage and speaking![1]

My "cohort" sisters, Angelise Schrader and Michele Clark, who formed a hedge of protection around me and prayed for me when doubt and weariness set in.

Pastor Steve King at Cherrydale Baptist Church for his kindness, encouragement, teaching, and wisdom.

The pastors and staff at Cherrydale Baptist Church. They are an incredible group of godly people. It is a joy and privilege to have them in my life.

My Bible study group, Cornerstone, who meet every Sunday morning. They welcomed me into the group with tremendous kindness and compassion.

Xulon Publishing, with special thanks to Freida Shingleton, Chris Shingleton and Marc Bermudez for their professionalism, support and patience.

There are so many more people who have encouraged me along the way, too numerous to mention. Just know I am deeply grateful and love you all.

Table of Contents

Introduction

The stories in this book are my "stones of remembrance." They are a record of the struggles and victories I have gone through, the insights and teachings I have gleaned along the way, and my personal testimony to the amazing grace of God.

In the Old Testament, the Israelites stacked stones as a reminder for current and future generations to always remember the miracles God had wrought on their behalf. They were markers of the events of their journey to the Promised Land.

When they arrived on the bank of the Jordan River, the Israelites were on the brink of witnessing one of His greatest promises coming to pass—a promise given way back in Abraham's day—that they would be freed from the confines of slavery and take possession of the Promised Land. Now God's message to them was, "Remember!"

The Lord instructed them to set up two stacks of stones, one in the middle of the river as they passed over into the Promised Land, and the second one at Gilgal, after the crossing.

> *Then Joshua set up twelve stones in the midst of the Jordan, in the place where the feet of the priests who bore the ark of the covenant stood; and they are there to this day (Joshua 4:9 NKJV).*

Now the people came up from the Jordan on the tenth day of the first month, and they camped in Gilgal on the east border of Jericho. And those twelve stones which they took out of the Jordan, Joshua set up in Gilgal. Then he spoke to the children of Israel, saying: "When your children ask their fathers in time to come, saying, 'What are these stones?' then you shall let your children know, saying, 'Israel crossed over this Jordan on dry land'; for the Lord your God dried up the waters of the Jordan before you until you had crossed over, as the Lord your God did to the Red Sea, which He dried up before us until we had crossed over (Joshua 4:19-23 NKJV).

The monument at Gilgal was a reminder that God had opened the river for them, just as He had opened the Red Sea for the previous generation to cross to safety as they escaped the Egyptians. The one in the river hidden beneath the water was a reminder that their past lives were now buried and gone.

The stories in this book are my stone stacks. I share them in the hope that perhaps something I have gone through may, in turn, give hope and encouragement to another, and that they too will come to know the God I know—not a religion but a Person, Jesus Christ.

1

An Anchor in My Soul

*This hope is a strong and trustworthy anchor for our souls.
It leads us through the curtain into God's inner sanctuary.
(Hebrews 6:19 NLT)*

Every journey has a beginning. My physical journey began on May 19, 1962 when I was born, but the most important journey, my spiritual one, began in 1972 at the age of ten.

That was the morning my dad died. I woke up, realizing something was not quite right. We lived in a house with old-fashioned wooden shutters which were closed every evening. By the angle of the light coming through the slats, I could judge the time of day. This morning, the light immediately told me the morning was advanced. My first thought was, "Yippee, Mom forgot to wake me for school. I get to stay home today!" That happy delusion rapidly dissipated. Hearing voices, I peeked out of my bedroom door and saw my mom, my aunt, a family friend, and our doctor standing together talking in hushed tones.

My dad had been seriously injured in a car crash a couple of months earlier. He survived the crash but came out of the wreck with a bad contusion on his head. A short time later, a blood clot passed through his body and, when it reached his brain, the damage was done. He no longer recognized my sister or myself, only my mom. He was sent home when the hospital could do no more for him. It was simply a matter of time before he passed, but none of us had grasped that.

They must have heard the door open because, shortly afterwards, my aunt came into my bedroom. She sat on my bed, put her arms around me and said, "Your dad has gone to join gentle Jesus." With that simple statement, my life changed forever.

After my aunt left the room, the next person who arrived on the scene was my seventeen-year old sister who took charge authoritatively and decisively. She told me not to cry and to stay away from our mom who had so much to deal with right then. Before anyone thinks badly of my poor sister, she was simply trying to be an adult and take care of our mother. I cannot imagine what she must have been going through. Unlike me, she was extremely close to my father and must have been devastated. She marched me off to the corner store with her to buy a loaf of bread. I obeyed, confused and bewildered, unaware the Bread of Life was about to reach out to me.

After we got back, I was left to my own devices. I corralled my dogs and wandered off to my playroom, a lost, lonely, desperately confused little girl with no-one to turn to. I loved reading and had a bookshelf crammed with books. For the first time, I noticed a Bible and a strange impulse made me pull it out. It fell open and I looked down to read John 3:16.

> *For God so loved the world that He gave His only-begotten Son, that whosoever shall believe in Him shall not perish but have everlasting life (John 3:16 NKJV).*

As I read that verse, something stirred in my spirit. No angels appeared, no heavenly choirs sang, light did not flood the room, but quietly and gently, a small anchor was placed deep within my soul, the other end tethered securely to Him.

It took another fifteen years before I accepted Christ, but that anchor and tether held me firmly through times of struggle and loss until the time came for me to start walking with Him and fulfilling His plan for my life.

2
Saved from the Pit

I was sliding down into the pit of death, and he pulled me out.
He brought me up out of the mud and dirt. He set my feet on a rock.
He gave me a firm place to stand on.
(Psalm 40:2 NIRV)

David authored this psalm. Fifteen years after my dad died, I found myself following in David's footsteps, sliding down into the pit of death. The darkness around me was pitch black with no glimmers of light. It was a horrific place to be.

In nature, predators always look for the weak, for those who have been separated from the group—that is the animal they stalk. That also is how Satan operates. He circles his prey waiting for the opportune moment to pounce. Paul described it perfectly when he wrote, *"your adversary the devil walks about like a roaring lion, seeking whom he may devour" (1 Peter 5:8 NKJV).*

I had moved to a new city to take up a new job. I was alone with no friends or family around me. To add to my misery, I was also carrying enormous guilt. I had married at age twenty and the relationship had sputtered out after two years. Looking back, I can now see I had married so young because I was looking for someone to love me and fill the aching void in my heart. Now, I was divorced and truly believing I had failed God. I was despairing over what I had done; I had taken vows and broken them.

One evening, in the solitude of my home, I reached breaking point. I cried out to God, telling Him I was going to take my own life because I couldn't handle the loneliness and trauma any longer. It wasn't that I wanted to die; I just wanted the pain to stop. I finally fell asleep exhausted.

I dragged myself into the office the next day, unaware God was about to pull on the tether He had anchored within me all those years ago. I was working for a recording studio, and one of the composers asked me to go for a walk with him because he needed to talk to me. I did not know him very well, so it all seemed a little weird, but I was too tired and washed out to question it. We went down to the nearby river and strolled along the bank. It was obvious he was extremely uncomfortable and really did not want to be there. He finally said he was just going to blurt it out and if I thought he was crazy, so be it.

He told me the evening before he had been in church and the Holy Spirit had told him I was contemplating taking my own life. He needed to tell me there was nothing I had done, or could ever do, that was so bad God would turn His back on me. He was waiting for me with open arms.

At that point, he stopped and looked at me pathetically. It was the same look my puppy gives me when she has done something on the carpet. "Say something, anything, please," my new friend implored. What I remember most about that moment was that there was no emotion, no choir of angels, no violins. I simply said, "Yep, you're right." That Sunday I went with him to church and accepted Christ. From that moment, my life changed and I started on a new adventure walking with Jesus.

I don't want to stop there, however, and have anyone think life became unicorns and rainbows for me. For the past thirty years, I have faced an ongoing battle with depression. But I now know when that dark cloud tries to settle over me, I will not descend into the pit. Instead, I will walk through the valley, and He will be walking with me every step of the way, holding my hand. He will bring me out safely on the other side.

If you are reading this, sitting in a deep, dark pit of despair, do not give into it and carry the hurt alone. If you have given up hope and feel there is no way out, that happiness and joy are a thing of the past, please, I beg of you, reach out to someone—a friend, a family member, someone at your church, a pastor. They will not think you are crazy. They will not think you are weak. They will feel blessed you trusted them enough to turn to them. God is still on His throne, He is still in heaven, but He uses His children as His instruments. I promise you, there is hope. It does get better; it will get better. I am living proof of that.

And to the others reading this, be sensitive to small signs of hurt in those around you and especially check in on your "strong" friends. Often it is the people who exhibit no outward signs that are in the most pain. We need to take care of each other.

3

The Heavens Declare the Glory of God

The heavens declare the glory of God;
The skies proclaim the work of his hands.
(Psalm 19:1 NIV)

When you are down on your knees crying out to God or curled up in the fetal position wondering how on earth you will ever be able to get to your feet again, find the strength to stand. When the heartache and pain is overwhelming, when hope is running perilously low, when all the forces of darkness seem to be arrayed against you, find the strength to stand. Stand and lift your eyes to the universe above.

> *Lift up your eyes on high, and see who has created these things, who brings out their host by number; He calls them all by name (Isaiah 40:26 NKJV).*

Look up and see the night sky *"proclaim the work of His hands."* Every star hung in that broad, inky blackness was placed there by Him and He knows each one by name.

"The heavens declare the glory of God," and they really do declare His glory. In movies, we watch enormous spaceships cross the vast expanse of space silently, but in reality, space is alive with sound. Every star, every planet, every comet, every asteroid, every constellation, pulsates with sound,

singing their praises to God. Billions of stars rotate endlessly, following their appointed paths, in absolute precision and perfect timing. Just as God controls the courses of the stars, He controls the course of our lives.

> *You saw me before I was born. Every day of my life was recorded in your book. Every moment was laid out before a single day passed (Psalm 139:16 NLT).*

For a small glimpse of the immenseness of His universe, ponder these facts:

- Light travels at 186,000 miles per second. A light year is how far light travels in one year. One light year equals 5.88 trillion miles (5,880,000,000,000). The most distant galaxy astronomers have been able to identify is thirteen billion light years away, or 13,000,000,000 x 5,880,000,000,000.[1]

- The Whirlpool Galaxy is thirty-one million light years away from Earth. Thirty-one million multiplied by 5.88 trillion is the distance you would need to cover to reach it. And it contains 300 billion stars.[2]

- According to NASA, there are approximately 10 billion galaxies in the observable universe, with probably, on average, 100 billion stars per galaxy. That translates to one billion trillion (1,000,000,000,000,000,000,000) stars in the observable universe. And that is only the "observable" universe. Who knows how many more billions there are out there?

> *When I consider your heavens, the work of your fingers, the moon and the stars, which you have set in place, what is mankind that you are mindful of them, human beings that you care for them? (Psalm 8:3-4 NIV).*

God has masterfully planned and ordered everything in all creation. You are part of His creation and He cares for you. And you think He can't handle your problem? Do you doubt He can't bring you through your heartache? Do you fear He cannot make something beautiful out of the mess of your life? Look up into the awe-inspiring beauty of His spectacular universe and take heart. He not only can, He will.

4

Fearfully and Wonderfully Made

I praise you because I am fearfully and wonderfully made.
(Psalm 139:14 NIV)

One of the current fads is to research your ancestry and discover your lineage. The internet is littered with sites offering DNA tests, and television is awash in Ancestry.com and 23andMe advertisements. You may find out who your ancestors are, but the tests will not call attention to the most important fact about your DNA.

There is only one you. Only one person in the billions walking the earth with your DNA. No one else has the same genetic makeup or the same fingerprints. You are unique. Your DNA is a miracle of God.

If you have any doubt you are not "fearfully and wonderfully" made, just stop and ponder that DNA. Starting with just four nucleotides (characters) your three billion-character DNA is formed. If stretched out, the DNA from one single cell would be six feet long. If you wanted to read your DNA, reading one character per second, night and day, it would take you ninety-six years.[1]

As if that isn't enough to prove your body is a miracle of creation, think about this. One hundred thousand miles of blood vessels link every living cell in your body.[2] The average adult human brain has around 100 billion neurons and 100,000 miles of blood vessels. The distance around the world at the equator is 24,900 miles.[3] There are 107,000,000 cells inside your eye alone.[4] It is difficult to calculate the total number of cells in the human body, but the latest calculation comes in at around 37.2 trillion. Written out that is 37,200,000,000,000![5]

> *For we are His workmanship, created in Christ Jesus for good works, which God prepared beforehand so that we should walk in them (Ephesians 2:10 NKJV).*

The Greek work for workmanship is *poiema*. We get our English words poem and poetry from it. We are God's poem—His work of art. C.S Lewis in *The Problem of Pain* wrote, "We are, not metaphorically, but in very truth, a divine work of art."[6]

Timothy Keller, founding pastor of Redeemer Presbyterian Church in Manhattan and best-selling author, wrote:

> "Do you know what it means that you are God's work-manship? What is art? Art is beautiful, art is valuable, and art is an expression of the inner being of the maker, of the artist. Imagine what that means. You're beautiful, you're valuable, and you're an expression of the very inner being of the Artist, the divine Artist, God Himself. Jesus is an Artist! And you are His crowning achievement, His masterpiece!"

> *My frame was not hidden from you, when I was being made in secret, intricately woven in the depths of the earth (Psalm 139:15 NRSV).*

You are not a cosmic accident. You are not a random collision of particles. You did not crawl out of the primordial sludge. Don't ever let feelings of inferiority overpower you. You are woven together like the finest silk tapestry. You are a walking miracle, designed by God Himself.

5

His Plan for Your Life

*You saw me before I was born. Every day of my life was recorded
in your book.
Every moment was laid out before a single day passed.
(Psalm 139:16 NLT)*

Have you ever questioned if God has a plan for you or if you are at the mercy of time and chance? Do you sometimes wander through life feeling like you are a piece of flotsam or jetsam being tossed around on the waves, seemingly going nowhere?

(By the way, there is a difference between flotsam and jetsam. Flotsam is the goods found floating on the sea resulting from a shipwreck. Jetsam is the things cast into the sea to lighten the load from a ship in danger of being wrecked. Whatever sinks is called lagan. I hadn't heard of lagan before writing this, but I know I don't want to be it!)

The good news is God has a unique plan for you. It was written long before you were even born, in eternity past. And it follows if He has a plan for your life, He wants you to know it.

To find out God's will and plan for you, there is a vital first step. You need to learn to recognize His voice. And the only way to do that is to read His Word.

*And when He brings out his own sheep, He goes before
them; and the sheep follow Him, for they know His voice
(John 10:4 NKJV).*

The next question that often comes up is "What happens if what I want
is different from what He wants? How does His plan gel with mine?"
When you align your will with His, He will put His desires in your heart.

*Many are the plans in a person's heart, but it is the Lord's
purpose that prevails (Proverbs 19:21 NIV).*

*We can make our plans, but the Lord determines our steps
(Proverbs 16:9 NLT).*

His will is His love. People are often terrified of asking God what His
will is for their life because they fear He might ask them to do something they dread. We don't need to fear. He loves us and whatever He
plans for us comes from His heart of love. He sent His precious Son to
die for us, nailed to a wooden cross on a barren hillside. How can we
doubt He will not do His best for us?

*I know the plans I have in mind for you, declares the Lord;
they are plans for peace, not disaster, to give you a future
filled with hope (Jeremiah 29:11 CEB).*

*No eye has seen, no ear has heard, and no mind has
imagined what God has prepared for those who love
Him (1 Corinthians 2:9 NLT).*

Our goal should be to stay within the boundaries of God's plan for us.
The only way to do that is to read His Word and seek His Spirit. He is
not trying to hide His plan from us. He will show you the way, step by
step, if you sincerely ask Him for His plan.

The Lord will work out His plans for my life – for your faithful love, O Lord, endures forever (Psalm 138:8 NLT).

"Trust the past to God's mercy, the present to God's love, and the future to God's providence" (St. Augustine).

6

Don't Avoid the Garden

In his anguish he prayed more earnestly,
and his sweat became like great drops of blood
falling down on the ground.
(Luke 22:44 NRSV)

Every now and then, I read something that pounds me between the eyes and changes my way of thinking about something. This is one. Don't try to avoid Gethsemane. Don't try to avoid the garden. Don't try to avoid hardship.

No one wants to go through pain and certainly no one wants to go through a "Garden of Gethsemane" experience like our Lord Jesus endured. But often it is in the garden, lying on cold stony ground, that we receive our greatest blessing.

Even Jesus had to pass through the anguish of Gethsemane as it was God's will for Him.

> Down shadowy lanes, across strange streams,
> Bridged over by our broken dreams;
> Behind the misty caps of years,
> Beyond the great salt fount of tears,
> The garden lies. Strive as you may,
> You cannot miss it in your way.

15

All paths that have been, or shall be,
Pass somewhere through Gethsemane.

All those who journey, soon or late,
Must pass within the garden gate;
Must kneel alone in darkness there,
And battle with some fierce despair.
God pity those who cannot say,
"Not mine, but thine," who only pray,
"Let this cup pass," and cannot see
The purpose in Gethsemane.
(Ella Wheeler Wilcox)

George Matheson described the garden experience beautifully in his book, Thoughts for Life's Journey:

> My soul reject not the place of your prostration. It has ever been your robing room for royalty. Ask the great ones of the past what has been the spot of their prosperity; they will say, "It was the cold ground on which I once was lying." Ask Abraham; he will point you to the sacrifice on Moriah. Ask Moses; he will date his fortune from his danger in the Nile. Ask Joseph; he will direct you to the dungeon. Ask Ruth; she will bid you build her monument in the field of her toil. Ask David; he will tell you that his songs came from the night. Ask Job; he will remind you that God answered him out of the whirlwind... Ask one more - the Son of Man... He will answer, "From the cold ground on which I was lying – the Gethsemane ground."

The hour of your loneliness will crown you. Your day of depression will regale you. It is your desert that will break forth into singing; it is trees of your silent forest that will clap their hands. The voice of God to your evening will be this, "Your treasure is hid in the ground where you were lying." [1]

Alexander Solzhenitsyn said: "It was only when I lay there on the rotting prison straw that I sensed within myself the first stirring of good. Gradually, it was disclosed to me that the line separating good and evil passes, not through states, nor between classes, nor between political parties either, but right through all human hearts. So, bless you, prison, for having been in my life." [2]

> *Before I was afflicted, I went astray, but now I obey Your Word. It was good for me to be afflicted so that I may learn your decrees (Psalm 119:67, 71 NIV).*

Your adversity and pain will become the bridge to a more intimate relationship with Him. He will come to you during these times if you let Him. Crises may try to crush you but God will use them to comfort, teach, and mold you further into the image of His beloved Son. Your period of despair and anguish will end, and, if you allow it, the experience can be the means by which God brings you to His greatest blessings.

> *And we know that all things work together for good to those who love God, to those who are the called according to His purpose (Romans 8:28 NKJV).*

7

Holy Hesitation

So then, my beloved brethren, let every man be swift to hear,
slow to speak, slow to wrath.
(James 1:19 NKJV)

A more complete title to my writing is "Holy Spirit Hesitation." I define this moment of hesitation as the pause that should occur between someone speaking and your answering to allow the Holy Spirit time to talk to your spirit and prevent you from sticking your foot in your mouth.

Credit for this idea goes to a wonderful man, Bob Kelso, who regularly teaches the Cornerstone Bible study group I attend on Sunday mornings. He spoke on this principle one morning and it really impacted me.

Someone said we more often listen with the intent to reply, not to hear. While the person is speaking, we are formulating our answer. Or, we respond impulsively or in anger when it is something we don't like to hear, behavior which in turn causes more drama and angst.

Instead, it is good to pause and give the Holy Spirit a chance to intervene.

A gentle answer turns away wrath, but a harsh word stirs
up anger (Proverbs 15:1 NIV).

*The tongue is a flame of fire. It is a whole world of wicked-
ness, corrupting your entire body. It can set your whole life
on fire, for it is set on fire by hell itself (James 3:6 NLT).*

I am sure the apostle Peter wished many times he had paused and thought
before impetuously opening his mouth. He once had the audacity to
rebuke Jesus. "*He spoke plainly about this, and Peter took him aside and
began to rebuke him. But when Jesus turned and looked at his disciples, he
rebuked Peter. 'Get behind me, Satan!' he said. "You do not have in mind
the concerns of God, but merely human concerns" (Mark 8:32-33 NIV).*

But then, in his defense, he did not have the Holy Spirit operating in
him at first. This anointment only came after Pentecost. But Peter did
have the living Lord standing by his side, giving him the "seriously dude?"
look whenever he blurted something out.

Peter also has the unenviable honor of being interrupted in mid-
speech by both God the Father and God the Son. On the mount of
Transfiguration, God the Father interrupted him while he was sug-
gesting the apostles build tabernacles for Jesus, Moses, and Elijah.

*Then Peter answered and said to Jesus, "Lord, it is good for
us to be here; if You wish, let us make here three tabernacles: one for You, one for Moses, and one for Elijah. While
he was still speaking, behold, a bright cloud overshadowed
them; and suddenly a voice came out of the cloud, saying,
"This is My beloved Son, in whom I am well pleased. Hear
Him! (Matthew 17: 4-5 NKJV).*

Jesus cut Peter off and told him, in no uncertain terms, to be quiet
when Peter tried to dissuade Jesus from going to the cross (see Mark
8:32-33 above).

Peter was probably also speaking when the Holy Spirit arrived at Pentecost. But Peter proclaimed one of the greatest truths in the Bible when he responded to Jesus' question, "Who do you say I am?"

> *Simon Peter answered, "You are the Messiah, the Son of the living God" (Matthew 16:16 NIV).*

The moral of the story is to pause and allow God to speak to you before you respond. That way the fruits of the Spirit will be evident in your life and you will spread peace not drama.

> *A person's words can be a source of wisdom, deep as the ocean, fresh as a flowing stream (Proverbs 18:4 NLT).*

8

Be Real

And when you pray, do not use vain repetitions as the heathen do.
For they think that they will be heard for their many words.
(Matthew 6:7 NKJV)

This is one of my pet peeves. Recently, I received yet another email from a fellow Christian filled to the brim with super-spiritual phrases. I am sure the person's heart was perfectly genuine, but can we please stop with the clichés and just be real?

Instead of saying "I'm lifting you in prayer to the Lord," can we not just say, "I am praying for you?" And almost every time someone says grace, out comes the worn-out phrase "bless this food to our bodies." Are we really thanking Him for the food or are we just parroting a phrase without thinking about the meaning?

You can imagine how delighted I was when I found out Christian pastor and author Charles Swindoll agreed with me and had the same peeve/plea. His list of clichés included "a time of food, fun, and fellowship," "just trust the Lord," and "bless the gift and the giver" among others.[1]

We represent a God who created a universe so enormous it has to be measured in light years. He created the tallest mountains and the deepest oceans. He filled those oceans with creatures like the blue whale, whose average size varies between 80 and 100 feet long and can weigh in at

200 tons. Its heart is the size of the average car.[2] The Lord's creativity is immense, and the best we can come up with are hackneyed, unimaginative, over-used, and worn out phrases?

Jesus told the Pharisees they were guilty of using meaningless repetition *(Matthew 6:7)*. Before we nod our heads and agree with Him, we should probably stop and consider ourselves. Are we not doing the same thing?

Worse of the worst is throwing "pat" doctrinal advice to someone who is suffering and then walking on, feeling we have done our Christian duty. Telling someone "the joy of the Lord is your strength" is not helpful when they are in pain and struggling to keep going. What they need during this time is for someone to sit quietly by their side and simply listen.

Can't we just be real? The world needs authentic Christians.

9

Are You Bug Spray or Air Freshener?

Words kill, words give life, they're either poison or fruit; you choose.
(Proverbs 18:21 MSG)

First, I cannot take credit for the brilliant title of this chapter. That honor goes to my senior pastor. I thought it was fantastic, so I "borrowed" it. Much catchier than "careless words create deep wounds," which was my original title.

While the title may be amusing, the subject is not. Careless, thoughtless, and cruel words can wound deeply and often leave lifetime scars. The tongue is an amazing organ – it can sweetly sing a baby to sleep and allow worshippers to raise their voices to God, but it can also spew vitriol, incite violence, and be used to destroy, divide, and discourage.

Publius, the Greek sage, said, "I have often regretted my speech, never my silence."

Words have immense power. Words bring life. A word spoken into someone's life at the right time could save them and give them hope to continue walking. Sometimes all it takes is a kind word and the gentle touch of the Holy Spirit to start the healing process.

A person's words can be a source of wisdom, deep as the
ocean, fresh as a flowing stream (Proverbs 18:4 NLT).

23

*Kind words are like honey – sweet to the soul and healthy
for the body (Proverbs 16:24 NLT).*

When you leave a room, do you leave behind a sweet aroma or a skunk-like odor? You've met those negative people. The ones with a critical spirit, who leave you feeling like you have just taken a bath in hydrochloric acid. It is just as easy to be kind and encouraging as it is to be cynical and critical.

*Your own soul is nourished when you are kind; it is
destroyed when you are cruel (Proverbs 11:17 TLB).*

It can sometimes take years to heal from wounds caused by careless words. Some never recover.

*Kind words heal and help; cutting words wound and
maim (Proverbs 15:4 MSG).*

How often has a thoughtless and cruel word driven someone away from church? Max Lucado recounts the story of a woman who had bravely fought the battle against alcoholism and started attending church. That was until she overheard someone ask, "Why is that drunk still hanging around the church." She was so wounded by those hateful words, she never returned.

Imagine a child on the receiving end of this comment, "Why can't you be more like your sister/brother?" Boom – insecurity and self-doubt are sown. Or a comment like, "She's the pretty one; her sister is the clever one." This can cause one sibling to grow up thinking her worth is only in her looks and her intelligence is limited. The other sibling could grow up thinking she looks like Quasimodo and needs to be kept in the belfry.

Often in the heat of the moment, we blurt out something we immediately regret. It helps to take deep breath and run the thought through your head before voicing it to prevent this. I am preaching to myself. Red hair and Scottish DNA make for a combustible combination. So, my prayer each day is, *"Lord put a guard about my tongue, and keep watch over the door of my lips" (Psalm 141:3).* I am most definitely a work in progress.

10

The Christian Country Club

*I do not pray that You should take them out of the world
but that You should keep them from the evil one.
(John 17:15 NKJV)*

God did not call us to form a Christian country club and hang out with only those like ourselves, separated from the outside world. If you never spend time in the real world, how can you ever reach the lost?

Too many Christians get saved and then settle down into a nice, comfortable lifestyle. They go to church on Sundays, to home groups and bible studies, and often work and play together. They become insulated, comfortable, believing they are serving God, and all is good. They are convinced God is giving them gold stars for their good behavior and piety. But they hardly ever touch the world outside of their Christian life, hardly ever meet people who are lost, in pain, in darkness, and are desperately in need of a Savior.

From *Outlive Your Life* by Max Lucado:

> When the Day of Pentecost had fully come, they were all with one accord in one place. (Acts 2:1) This is the earliest appearance of the church. Consider where God placed His people. Not isolated in a desert or quarantined in a bunker. Not separated from society, but

smack-dab in the center of it, in the heart of one of the largest cities at its busiest time.

We fall into the trap of ritual religion. Sunday church services, Wednesday evening prayer meetings, weekend retreats and believe we are serving God when in fact we are simply hanging out together making ourselves feel good. But where is the longing for Him? To know Him and "the power of His resurrection." [1]

We should be like Isaiah, *"Also I heard the voice of the Lord, saying, 'Whom shall I send, and who will go for Us?' Then I said, 'Here am I! Send me'" (Isaiah 6:8 NKJV).*

In his book, *The Pursuit of God,* A.W. Tozer writes:

Complacency is a deadly foe of all spiritual growth. Acute desires must be present or there will be no manifestation of Christ to His people. He waits to be wanted. Too bad that with many of us He waits so long, so very long, in vain. Every age has its own characteristics. Right now, we are in an age of religious complexity. The simplicity that is in Christ is rarely found among us. In its stead are programs, methods, organizations and a world of nervous activities which occupy time and attention but can never satisfy the longing of the heart. The shallowness of our inner experience, the hollowness of our worship and that servile imitation of the world that marks our promotional methods, all testify that we, in this day, know God only imperfectly, and the peace of God scarcely at all. [2]

We also need to be careful we do not become like the Pharisees, avoiding people because they are not like us. God wants us to show His love to the world just like His Son did, not withdraw into religious isolation.

He never intended his church to become an exclusive country club. He meant it to be an army on the march, striding into enemy territory, and reclaiming the land usurped by the Enemy.

> *Therefore, go and make disciples of all nations, baptizing them in the name of the Father and of the Son and of the Holy Spirit, and teaching them to obey everything I have commanded you. And surely, I am with you always, to the very end of the age (Matthew 28:19-20 NIV).*

11

Anxiety

Do not be anxious about anything, but in every situation,
by prayer and petition with thanksgiving, present your requests to God.
(Philippians 4:6 NIV)

A nxiety—that horrible, gnawing feeling in the pit of your stomach that churns up your insides. I had come through, or I thought I had come through, a horrible three-year period of loss, trauma, and change, but then, out of the blue, came the anxiety attacks. They struck always in the early hours of the morning, between three and five. I had never experienced anything like this before - waking up to a sense of impending doom and darkness. And I knew it wasn't rational. I had no reason to feel this way.

The situation grew worse when I started waking up in the night in fear of the impending anxiety attack. So, I was now anxious about getting anxious! Awesome—just what I needed to complete the miserable picture. Anxiety has a nasty habit of bringing its companions along—panic, fear, and dread. An unholy trinity of misery.

I soon discovered I was not the only one dealing with this issue. People around me were going through, or had gone through, the same thing but were too scared to speak out or ask for help because they thought they would be perceived as weak or neurotic. It's a dark valley to walk through alone, so I decided I needed to share my experience.

29

The good news is we are not walking through the valley alone. God is right there with us, leading us through and bringing us out. He brings us THROUGH the valley—THROUGH. He doesn't leave us in it.

> *Even though I walk through the darkest valley, I will fear no evil, for you are with me; your rod and your staff, they comfort me (Psalm 23:4 NIV).*

But it won't be without a battle. The Enemy wants you to think you are a weak Christian because you are not standing on the Word and overcoming the situation, that it is never going to end, that you are always going to feel that way, that you're going crazy. Those are all lies. Jesus warned us that Satan is "the father of lies." And he is darned good at lying. He has had eons to perfect his craft. But the good news is he is a defeated enemy. He was defeated decisively and permanently at the cross. The victory is already won. Jesus did it for you.

God knows we are going to struggle with anxiety; that it will come at some point in our lives. If He did not anticipate this occurring within us, He would not have put so many scriptures about anxiety in His word.

> *When anxiety was great within me, your consolation brought me joy (Psalm 94:19 NIV).*

Even Jesus battled with anxiety. Look at His lonely figure in the garden of Gethsemane, on His knees in agony, sweating blood, and asking God to take the cup away from Him. But He entrusted His fears to His Heavenly Father and His Father brought Him through.

I wish I could tell you my personal battle was won in an instant. It wasn't. It took time. The attacks grew less and less intense, and the time span between them grew longer. The prescription that worked for me was listening to praise and worship music in the dark early morning hours and holding onto scripture when the cloud descended.

At the beginning, when the attacks were severe, I also accepted help in the form of medication which took the edge off and allowed me to sleep. You need to get rest because exhaustion just makes the situation worse. I was able to stop taking the medication as things improved.

Don't be super-spiritual about getting medical help. Sometimes it is needed. Whichever path you choose, medication or no medication, do not heap condemnation on those who follow the other path. Do what is needed in your situation.

There is one thing I do know, and I have absolutely no doubt about this. He brought me through it, and He will bring you through it too. There is light at the end of your tunnel. Just keep walking, clinging to His hand, and you will emerge into the sunshine again.

> *So, do not fear, for I am with you; do not be dismayed, for I am your God. I will strengthen you and help you; I will uphold you with my righteous right hand (Isaiah 41:10 NIV).*

> *Peace I leave with you; my peace I give you. I do not give to you as the world gives. Do not let your hearts be troubled and do not be afraid (John 14:27 NIV).*

12

In the Shade of the Juniper Tree

But he himself traveled a day's journey into the wilderness, and he came and sat down under a juniper tree and asked [God] that he might die. He said, "It is enough; now, O Lord, take my life, for I am no better than my fathers.
(1 Kings 19:4 AMP)

I hope this doesn't happen to anyone reading this but there is an excellent chance that at some point in your life you will reach a point of total exhaustion—physically, mentally, emotionally, and spiritually. You may feel like you just want to give up. Your friends may helpfully throw scripture at you. Thank them and save the scriptures for later, when you are strong enough to stand on them.

The story of the prophet Elijah is an example of how God deals with the exhausted, the overwhelmed, the ones despairing, because they are exhausted from standing or walking or sitting or believing.

Elijah had just come from a major victory over the Baal prophets. To prove God was the true God of Israel, Elijah called down fire from heaven to consume the sacrifice on the altar, an act the pagan Baals were unable to duplicate. He then commanded the Baal prophets to be put to death, which infuriated Jezebel, the queen of Israel, and a Baal follower. Breathing threats of murder and mayhem, she sent her henchmen to find

Elijah, who took off at high speed. One minute, he was an invincible prophet of God, the next one a normal, fallible human being.

"Be as watchful after the victory as before the battle"
(Andrew Bonar, Minister, Free Church of Scotland).

Whenever you have a major spiritual victory, watch out. This is often the time when you get caught with your guard down and then comes the plunge. There is a phenomenon known as "post event depression," that results from the withdrawal of stress hormones. Having been involved in the planning and preparation of many events in my work life, I know how the long hours and stress can affect people. The adrenalin and excitement keep the momentum going, and then, after the event, the emotional and physical crash comes. Usually the next day, a bunch of tired, cranky, depressed people arrive at the office and wander aimlessly around, growling at each other. The best solution is always food, rest, and then getting back to work.

Elijah was so depressed he asked God to take his life. I don't think any of our staff ever reached this point although they occasionally threatened each other's lives.

When Elijah begged God to remove him from the world, God didn't smack him upside the head or tell him to get a grip and hold onto scripture. Instead, He handled him gently and kindly. He encouraged the prophet to rest, catered a meal via an angel, and helped him get his eyes off the situation and back onto his Lord.

When someone has reached the point of exhaustion where they just can't face taking one more step, quite often what is needed are simple practical steps. Rest—physical and mental —is usually the first order of the day, followed by sustenance. Stressed, overwhelmed people seldom make good food choices. Sometimes appetites simply disappear, and people barely eat at all.

Once the physical has been taken care of, the next step is to spend quality time with the Savior. Not digging into the deep things of God but just enjoying His presence and spending time with Him. This is the best prescription to emerge refreshed and ready to face the next challenge.

> *But those who wait on the Lord shall renew their strength; they shall mount up with wings like eagles, they shall run and not be weary, they shall walk and not faint (Isaiah 40:31 NKJV).*

13

Sad Saturday

And Jesus cried out with a loud voice, and breathed His last.
(Mark 15:37 NKJV)

But he said to them, "Do not be alarmed. You seek Jesus of Nazareth,
who was crucified. He has risen!"
(Mark 16:6 NIV)

I s it Saturday for you—the time after the incident that took your feet out from under you, leaving you lying bleeding on the floor, bewildered and in pain?

Remember after Good Friday came Saturday. The disciples had to face a dark terrifying time. Their hopes and dreams had died on a wooden cross on a barren hill the day before. Now they faced Saturday, with nothing but sorrow and disappointment filling their hearts. They must have wandered around numb, in shock and disbelief. What they did not know was that resurrection Sunday was on its way.

Saturday can be the longest, toughest day to face. After your hopes and dreams have crashed and burned, after the dreaded medical diagnosis, after the confirmation of barrenness, after the betrayal by a spouse, after the abandonment by a friend, after the death of a loved one, comes the dark night of the soul—the somber walk of pain, confusion, and bewilderment. We all experience a Saturday at some point in our lives, and it may feel like it is dragging on with seemingly no end in sight.

But unlike the disciples on that Saturday, we know for sure that after Good Friday and sad Saturday came resurrection Sunday. While it may seem that Saturday will never end, it will.

Don't give up, keep walking, clinging to His Hand and His Word. I promise you resurrection Sunday is coming!

14

He Cares About the Little Things

Are not five sparrows sold for two copper coins?
And not one of them is forgotten before God.
But the very hairs of your head are all numbered.
Do not fear therefore; you are of more value than many sparrows.
(Luke 12:6-7 NKJV)

I have a propensity to feel bad when I go to God about something that, in the big scheme of things, I feel is small and insignificant. I am almost embarrassed to ask Him for help. After all, there are so many people out there in the world who are experiencing real tragedy and suffering.

There is no reason, however, for us to feel bad about going to Him. God understands the daily grind and the small nits can wear you to a frazzle. That the co-workers at the great job He gave you are standing on your last nerve. That the child you prayed and believed for and were so grateful to Him for giving to you is now a teenager driving you batty. (That boarding school in the remote Scottish Highlands is starting to look really good.) That the husband you adore is a one-man wrecking machine, leaving wet towels on the bathroom floor and dirty dishes in the sink. (Maybe he needs to join the teenager in the Scottish Highlands.)

When your child comes to you in tears because she has lost her favorite toy, you don't tell her there are children in refugee camps who have no toys and she should be grateful for the ones she has. No, you wipe away her tears and comfort her and help her find her "Puppy Love" stuffed dog.

God feels the same way about us. He is our Abba Father. He wants to help us in our small day-to-day struggles. So, never hesitate about taking them to Him, and His peace, which exceeds anything we can ever understand, will guard your heart and mind *(Philippians 4:7).*

15

The Opening Scene

These hard times are small potatoes compared to the coming good times,
the lavish celebration prepared for us.
There's far more here than meets the eye.
The things we see now are here today, gone tomorrow.
But the things we can't see now will last forever.
(2 Corinthians 4:16-18 MSG)

The lights dim and we snuggle down deeper into our seats, popcorn clutched in our hands, gazing up at the big screen anticipating the adventure to come. Sweeping music swells and the first scene unfolds. Indiana Jones is about to enthrall us with another adventure and, of course, being Indy, he always triumphs over his enemies.

We know the first scene in the movie is not the only scene we are going to view, that there is a whole lot more to come. The same applies to life.

Some are born into this world with a silver spoon in their mouths. Others are born into a world of struggle, their lives an uphill battle with few advantages. Infirmities or disabilities may be part of the challenge. The bases seem loaded against them.

However, our time on earth is brief and only a small fraction of our story, which started long before we were born.

Before I formed you in the womb, I knew you (Jeremiah 1:5 NKJV).

And we will be spending eternity with Him in heaven.

The free gift of God is eternal life through Jesus Christ our Lord (Romans 6:23 TLB).

Sandwiched in between those two eternal spaces of time is our life here on earth. If we view life through that lens, it takes on a different perspective. Pain and suffering are only for a brief season in the vast expanse of time. We can take courage, therefore, that this is earthly life is not the end. Heartache, tears, and pain will be erased. There is a brilliant future awaiting us.

He will wipe every tear from their eyes. There will be no more death or mourning or crying or pain, for the old order of things has passed away (Revelation 21:4 NIV).

Our life on earth is simply the opening scene in the sweeping saga of our lives. There is so much more to come. We need to keep walking. Eternity with the Father lies ahead of us.

16

Doubt vs. Unbelief

At that the boy's father cried out, "I have faith; help my lack of faith!"
(Mark 9:24 CEB)

There is a vast difference between doubt and unbelief. Unbelief is a matter of the will. It causes people to rebel against God. No matter what He does or says, they will not obey. Doubt is a matter of the heart and emotions. Doubt is experienced when a person waivers between fear and disbelief. The doubter says, "Lord, help my unbelief." The unbeliever says, "I will not believe."

In many translations, the word "unbelief" is used in this verse: *"Immediately the father of the child cried out and said with tears, Lord, I believe; help my unbelief!"* I believe a better translation is the one above. The man was not in willful unbelief. He was just struggling to find faith.

Unbelief is sin. Doubt (sincerely questioning God) is not. Abraham, Moses, and David all struggled to understand God. If you are asking honest questions, God will not turn away from you.

Doubt can be good. I am sure this statement will make some people gasp and think it is utter heresy but hear me out. I have always struggled with terrible feelings of failure and faithlessness when I had moments of doubt. I never ever doubted the existence of God or that Jesus came to earth and died for me. But sometimes doubts would creep in during my day-to-day walk. It was then I would question whether He really was hearing my prayers and if He was still working on my behalf.

So, when I read this in *Reason for God* by Timothy Keller, it gave me great comfort.

> A faith without some doubts is like a human body without any antibodies in it. People who blithely go through life too busy or indifferent to ask hard questions about why they believe as they do will find themselves defenseless against either the experience of tragedy or the probing questions of a smart skeptic. A person's faith can collapse almost overnight if she has failed over the years to listen patiently to her own doubts, which should only be discarded after long reflection.[1]

We are human. We are not perfect, and we walk in a fallen world. Jesus knows what it is like to walk on the earth and face human trials. This is one of the reasons He came to earth—so He could fully experience the trials and struggles we face and become our Advocate in heaven.

Jesus never castigated the person with doubt. Instead, He gently met the person at the point of their faith. A mustard seed is one of the smallest seeds on earth but it grows into one of the greatest trees. Jesus said all we needed was a small amount of faith on par with that of the tiny mustard seed and we would be able to move mountains.

> *So the Lord said, "If you have faith as a mustard seed, you can say to this mulberry tree, 'Be pulled up by the roots and be planted in the sea,' and it would obey you" (Luke 17:6 NKJV).*

The disciple Thomas is an excellent example of honest doubt.

> *"So he said to them, 'Unless I see in His hands the print of the nails, and put my finger into the print of the nails, and put my hand into His side, I will not believe'" (John 20:25 NKJV).*

He was not doubting out of rebellion; he was doubting out of disappointment and sorrow. And Jesus appeared to him personally and showed Thomas the evidence he was requesting.

> *Then he said to Thomas, "Put your finger here; see my hands. Reach out your hand and put it into my side. Stop doubting and believe" (John 20:27 NIV).*

Jesus healed the son of the father who cried out to Him, "Help my unbelief!" God comforted Job and rebuked his friends. And Jesus reached out to John the Baptist when John was in prison and starting to wonder if he had been wrong about Jesus being the Messiah.

> *Jesus answered and said to them, "Go and tell John the things which you hear and see: The blind see and the lame walk; the lepers are cleansed and the deaf hear; the dead are raised up and the poor have the gospel preached to them" (Matthew 11:4-5 NKJV).*

God is not limited by imperfect faith. Even the strongest faith is often mixed with an element of doubt. If you are struggling with doubts, go straight to God and He will meet you at your point of need.

17

Work with What You Have

So, when they were filled, He said to His disciples, "Gather up the fragments that remain, so that nothing is lost."
Therefore, they gathered them up, and filled twelve baskets with the fragments of the five barley loaves
which were left over by those who had eaten.
(John 6:12-13 NKJV)

We all know the story of the 5,000 people who came to hear Jesus preach. After He had spoken, He asked His disciples, "Where shall we buy bread, that these may eat?" The disciples were more than a little taken back. Seriously, where did He expect them to get food for 5,000 people? Apparently, the disciples had already forgotten the miracles they had seen Him do. We know how the story ends. Jesus took five loaves and two fish and fed the multitude.

The story of the 5,000 demonstrates how much God can do with just a little. It is important to note Jesus did not do something from nothing, although He could have. Instead, He took what the disciples had and worked with that.

So often we are overwhelmed by challenges in life, including the needs of others. In these moments, sometimes anxiety takes hold. We might think how on earth can we help? What can we say? Do we have sufficient knowledge to speak into someone's life? What happens if they ask a question we can't answer? What, if like me, you are shy and the thought of speaking out to someone about your faith curls your toes?

All Jesus needs us to do is to take a little step with the little we have, be it physical or spiritual, and He will go to work. When He takes anything, no matter how small, it becomes a blessing. So, offer your meager resources, whatever they are, and watch His miracle-working power spring into action.

18

Baby Steps vs. Big Steps

The steps of a good man are ordered by the Lord,
and he delights in his way.
(Psalm 37:23 NKJV)

We all know our walk is a walk of faith. *"We walk by faith not by sight" (2 Corinthians 5:7 NKJV)*. Our walks, however, are not all the same. God did not use a cookie cutter when He created us. He made us all different. *"I praise you, for I am fearfully and wonderfully made" (Psalm 139:14 NKJV)*. We have different life experiences, different personalities, we express emotion differently, we process life differently. Therefore, it follows that our walks, too, will be different.

A baby step of faith for me might be a giant step for someone else. Vice versa, something I view as a giant step for me could be a baby step of faith for someone else. The bottom line is we should never judge another person by how they are handling a situation. To us it may seem easy, to them it could be overwhelming and anxiety-inducing. And in turn, we might get frustrated with friends who don't seem to understand how frightening something is for us.

Our comfort comes from knowing, no matter whether it is a large step of faith or a teeny tiny one, God is right there with us, guiding us, supporting us, and making sure we don't fall and get hurt. Just as an earthly Dad walks carefully beside his child, ready to catch him or her should a stumble occur, so God walks alongside us, holding our hand as we take each step.

And no matter how small or large, God is proud of every step we take.

> *A man's heart plans his way, but the Lord directs his steps (Proverbs 16:9 NKJV).*

19

Why Is It So Hard to Pray?

*Now in the morning, having risen a long while before daylight,
He went out and departed to a solitary place; and there He prayed.
(Mark 1:35 NKJV)*

Why do so many of us struggle with prayer? It often seems so mysterious and difficult. We agonize over the right words, our minds wander, we fall asleep, we start off well and then lose the thread.

One of the reasons for this is there is a fallen angel walking the earth seeking those he may devour. Satan pays attention to us when we go to church, when we read spiritual books, when we attend Bible study, but he really pays attention when we pray because he knows what prayer does to his kingdom. It decimates it!

Throughout the books of Acts, you see prayer in action. Prison doors fly open, chains fall off, demons are cast out. Satan knows how powerful prayer is and he will do anything to stop it.

We also create our own hindrances to prayer. We wrestle to find the words we feel are appropriate. We wonder if we are praying hard enough. Should we be crying and sweating up a storm? We wonder if our prayer pose is correct. Should we be lying on the floor begging Him to hear us or kneeling with hands clasped in front of us with a beatifical look on our face?

There is no reason to stress about prayer. In its purest sense, it is simply a conversation with God.

We also do not need to speak in King James English. I have heard so many people switch over to King James "speak" when praying, which I personally find somewhat strange. I don't believe God talks like that. He was around way before the King James Bible was compiled so why would He use that language? We also don't need fancy words or flowery phrases. Some of my most heartfelt prayers have been extremely short, such as "Help, Lord!" or even more simple, 'Help!"

Prayer is an indispensable part of our Christian walk. If you want to know how vital prayer is, look to our perfect example of prayer in action. Jesus often withdrew from the crowds to a place of solitude to pray. If He thought prayer was that important, then so should we.

Mark wrote his gospel with the Romans as his target audience. The Romans were a no-nonsense people; action and power appealed to them. In chapter one, it is one exciting event after another. Jesus begins His Galilean ministry; calls His first four disciples, Peter, Andrew, James and John; casts out a slew of unclean spirits and demons; heals many; and preaches in the synagogue. Then, a small seemingly insignificant verse (Mark 1:35) is dropped into the middle of all the activity. Jesus went out to a solitary place to pray. That tiny verse is hugely important. Amid all the excitement, Jesus took time to pray. And we should too.

God loves to hear from His children. Find a quiet place, put aside the distractions, and simply pour your heart out to Him. He is ready and waiting to hear from you.

> *Base your happiness on your hope in Christ. When trials*
> *come endure them patiently; steadfastly maintain the*
> *habit of prayer (Romans 12:12 PHILLIPS).*

20

Oops, I Did it Again!

For I do not understand my own actions
[I am baffled and bewildered by them].
I do not practice what I want to do, but I am doing the very thing I hate
[and yielding to my human nature, my worldliness—my sinful capacity].
(Romans 7:15 AMP)

Don't you just hate it when you do the very thing you know you shouldn't do? We want to do the right thing, we know what the right thing is, but we still do the wrong thing.

You decide you are not going to lose your temper any more, you are not going to allow that annoying person to get under your skin, you are not going to have that second/third piece of chocolate cake. However, you can't seem to help yourself—you do it again. That bad habit or personality trait you want to overcome keeps rearing its ugly head, like a demonic critter from a Stephen King novel. Mine is a quick temper. I can blame my ancestry, those pesky Scots, or my red hair, but I know this is a lame excuse.

It gives me great comfort to know that Paul struggled with the same issue. Paul was human and, like us, he too struggled with sin. He sincerely desired in his heart to live up to God's standards and yet he failed again and again. Paul was facing the Christian dilemma of wanting to please God but still dealing with his unredeemed humanness. After we accept Christ, sin no longer reigns in our lives, but it still survives. That's why we have to ask Jesus to take control of our lives so our old habits and patterns of behavior can be broken. He told us we needed to abide in Him because we cannot walk the Christian walk in our own strength.

> *I am the vine; you are the branches. If you remain in Me*
> *and I in you, you will bear much fruit; apart from Me you*
> *can do nothing (John 15:5 NIV).*

Justification occurs at the moment we accept Christ, but sanctification takes a lifetime. Alan Redpath (British evangelist, pastor and author) said it this way, "It takes but a moment to make a convert, it takes a lifetime to manufacture a saint."

The one habit I've had to learn to break is to stop revisiting past sins. I know, beyond a shadow of doubt, Jesus died for my sins—past, present, and future—and I am washed clean by His blood. But in the past, I had trouble leaving those sins at the cross. I kept going back and retrieving them. I would confess my sins and take them to the cross, then remember them, feel guilty all over again, and retrieve them. I would take them back to the cross, confess them all over again, remember them, retrieve them, and feel guilty all over again. This pathetic, exhausting cycle would continue. I had my sins attached to a yo-yo. It was only when I fully understood grace and that He died for my sins, ALL my sins, that I was finally able to leave them at the foot of the cross.

> *For God was in Christ reconciling the world to Himself, no*
> *longer counting people's sins against them (2 Corinthians*
> *5:19 NLT).*

God doesn't count your sins against you, so why do you? The Creator of heaven and earth says they are no more, so let them go and don't allow the Enemy to bring them back to your remembrance. If he tries, just quote God's word right back at him.

> *I will be merciful when they fail, and I will erase their sins and wicked acts out of My memory as though they had never existed (Hebrews 8:12 VOICE).*

> *No matter how deep the stain of your sins, I can take it out and make you as clean as freshly fallen snow (Isaiah 1:18 TLB).*

Take your sins to the foot of the cross and leave them there. Step back, take a deep breath, and watch the blood flow down, washing them away. They are gone; He remembers them no more.

> Sometimes we breath in Christ's work on the Cross in tiny, stifled breaths. We thank Him for forgiving this sin, that fault, this situation. God wants us to take a full, deep, restorative breath. One that covers all of life— every past, present or future mistake. When Christ returned us to God's favor, God completely blotted out every sin (Anonymous).

21

No Scars?

They pierced My hands and My feet.
(Psalm 22:16 NKJV)

If you are a Christian and you tell me you have no scars, my response is going to be two-fold: 1) you are very blessed, and 2) what planet are you from?

We all have scars. Some are caused simply because we walk in a fallen, sinful world. Others are a result of trials sent by God to test us. We also sometimes inflict scars on ourselves by being disobedient to God, and then there are those we get by following Christ. Paul knew the reality of the latter.

> *From now on, let no one cause me trouble, for I bear on my*
> *body the marks of Jesus (Galatians 6:17 NIV).*

A Christian without scars begets the question, "Are you truly following Christ?" If you have somehow miraculously avoided scars in your life, you will undoubtedly acquire them at some point.

> *No wound? No scar?*
> *Yes, as the Master shall the servant be,*
> *And pierced are the feet that follow Me;*
> *But thine are whole: can he have followed far,*
> *Who has no wound nor scar?*
> *(Amy Carmichael, Missionary)*

53

Matthew West has a song called *The Healing Has Begun*, and the words perfectly describe why our scars are important. "There's a world of people dying from broken hearts, holding onto their guilt thinking they fell too far, so don't be afraid to show them your beautiful scars."[1]

Scars allow you to walk in someone's shoes, to be able to get down in the pit with them, to truly understand what they are going through, and to be able to help them walk out.

No matter how you came by your scars, be proud of them. Don't be afraid to show them to world. They are proof God heals.

22

Every Tear is Precious

You have seen me tossing and turning through the night.
You have collected all my tears and preserved them in your bottle!
You have recorded every one in your book.
(Psalm 56:8 TLB)

Tears are the way our body releases stress, grief, anxiety, and frustration. There are three types of tears: continuous, reflex, and healing. Continuous keeps our eyes lubricated, reflex cleans out foreign particles like dust and allergens, and emotional tears release stress hormones, which is why we often feel calmer and more relaxed after a good cry.[1] There is tremendous healing power in tears.

When emotional tears flow from pain and anguish, we sometimes wonder if He really sees our pain, if He really cares. Often, we ask, "Where are you, Lord?"

But God is always right by our side. He sees every tear we weep, and He holds each one close to His heart. David said, *"The Lord has heard the voice of my weeping"* (Psalm 6:8 NKJV). A single teardrop is enough to summon the King of Kings to your side.

"Jesus wept." This is the shortest verse in the Bible (well, in English anyway; there are two shorter ones if you read them in Greek). At the tomb of Lazarus, the Lord wept. Not because Lazarus was dead. He knew He

was moments away from raising Him from the dead. He wept for the heartache of the sisters and for the pain and death that sin had brought into this world.

Jeremiah, the weeping prophet, shows us the value God puts on tears. He was one of God's greatest prophets, but also one with the softest of hearts. He shed so many tears over Israel, God must have a few hundred bottles holding them.

I believe the one set of tears that must have been particularly precious to the Lord were the tears wept by His anguished, broken disciple, Peter, when Peter realized had betrayed his Friend and Lord.

Tears are as necessary for our spiritual growth as water is to grow seeds into plants. Tears will make you into a stronger Christian and, more than likely, a kinder, more understanding one. So go ahead and weep. Ignore anyone who tries to tell you it is a sign of weakness. Just point them to David, Jeremiah, Peter, and Jesus, and tell them you are in great company.

23

It is Well with My Soul

And the peace of God which surpasses all understanding,
will guard your hearts and minds through Christ Jesus.
(Philippians 4:7 NKJV)

The song "It is Well with My Soul" was written by Horatio G. Spafford in 1873. He was a successful lawyer and businessman who lived in Chicago with his wife and five children. His life, however, was marked by tragedy.

In 1871, his only son died at age four from pneumonia. In the same year, the Great Chicago Fire destroyed most of his business. He planned a European trip for his family in 1873 but had to remain behind to finish up some work; he encouraged his wife and daughters to go ahead without him. While crossing the Atlantic, on November 21, 1873, the ocean liner they were traveling on collided with another ship. It sank in about twelve minutes and the only member of his family to survive was his wife. His four daughters perished in the cold ocean. His wife sent Horatio a telegram, which said, "Saved alone." He later framed the telegram and kept it in his office.[1]

One of the ship's survivors said they heard his wife, Anna, saying, "God gave me four daughters. Now they have been taken from me. Someday I will understand why."

Horatio booked passage on the next available ship to
go to his wife. It is said he wrote *It is Well with My
Soul* while on this journey (excerpt below).

When peace, like a river, attendeth my way,
When sorrows like sea billows roll;
Whatever my lot, Thou hast taught me to say,
It is well, it is well with my soul.

Though Satan should buffet, though trials
should come,
Let this blest assurance control,
That Christ hath regarded my helpless estate,
And hath shed His own blood for my soul.

My sin, oh the bliss of this glorious thought!
My sin, not in part but the whole,
Is nailed to His cross, and I bear it no more,
Praise the Lord, praise the Lord, O my soul!

For me, be it Christ, be it Christ hence to live:
If Jordan above me shall roll,
No pain shall be mine, for in death as in life
Thou wilt whisper Thy peace to my soul.

I pray none of us ever has to go through this much heartbreak and pain,
but how amazing that, amid his suffering, Horatio Spafford still held
on to his God and wrote this incredibly beautiful and powerful song.
May we too follow his example and cling to God because He will always
bring us through, no matter how deep the anguish.

24

My Anchor Held

He stilled the storm to a whisper; the waves of the sea were hushed.
They were glad when it grew calm, and He guided them to their
desired haven.
(Psalm 107:29-30 NIV)

I have just come through a storm that seemed never ending. At times, it reached hurricane strength, and I wondered how I would ever hold on.

The seas have calmed now, and the waves have hushed. The waters are still choppy, the boat is still rocking, the wind is still blowing, but it is no longer at gale force. I am wet, battered, and bruised but I have come through. I can see my haven ahead, a harbor of peace and calm, secure in His love.

The best part? My little rowboat's anchor to my heavenly Father held through it all. When the storm was raging, and the waves were pounding down, and I could barely focus from the water and wind in my face, the one thing I could see throughout it all, albeit it sometimes only dimly, was the connection to my Anchor holding tight through it all.

We have this hope as an anchor for the soul, firm and
secure. It enters the inner sanctuary behind the curtain,

where our forerunner, Jesus, has entered on our behalf (Hebrews 6:19-20 NIV).

I did not write this to say, "Hey look at me! I came through!" I wrote this to say, "Hey look at me! He brought me through!" And if He did it for me, He will do it for you. So if you are currently adrift in a stormy sea and your boat is rocking wildly, please don't quit, please don't give up. He will come to you. He may even come to you walking on the water.

25

When You are Out of Oomph

But those who hope in the Lord will renew their strength.
They will soar on wings like eagles;
they will run and not grow weary;
they will walk and not be faint.
(Isaiah 40:31 NKJV)

There was a period when I was one tired, weary person. I was in what seemed like a never-ending valley. I knew that it was simply a valley; that He was walking with me, holding my hand; and that He would bring me out to the other side as He always did, but I was out of "oomph."

My energy was gone. I was trying to hold on to hope, but my fingernails were bloody and my arms were tired. I wasn't upset or sad. I was too tired to even feel those emotions. Those take effort; I was too weary for even that.

The months kept dragging on with no breakthrough. Finally, I ran into a spiritual brick wall and collapsed in a heap. I had reached the point where I felt utterly incapable of taking one more step. And if anyone had told me that *"the joy of the Lord was my strength,"* I might have come unglued.

Then reading a daily journal, I came across a piece on waiting and Isaiah 40:31. The writer explained that waiting is not a passive action, it is active. While we wait in hope and positive anticipation, God is working on our behalf. But the waiting can become tiring, especially when the days drag on and no movement is seen. That is when we need to stand on Isaiah 40:31 and claim His promise of new strength.

So I went to my Bible and read the verse, *"But those who hope in the Lord will renew their strength. They will soar on wings like eagles; they will run and not grow weary, they will walk and not be faint."*

My response? "Lord, You have got to be kidding! Run...walk...my knees are shaking they are so weak. I can barely walk, and I certainly cannot run." I felt like the albatross in the Disney animated movie, "The Rescuers," who needed a super long runway to take off. He would run wobbling from side to side, struggling to gain enough speed to take flight. He crashed a lot. His landings were even worse.

I spent a few more days moping along, dragging myself out of bed each morning, mad at myself for not standing more strongly, apologizing to Him every night for being weak. And as always, He treated me gently and kindly with no condemnation, just love.

The one thing I did, no matter how bad I felt, was to have my quiet time each day. It was so tempting to skip it, but I knew that was the worst thing I could do. Sometimes it felt like the words were falling on stony ground, but, more often than not, the Holy Spirit led me to comforting scriptures to help me hold on.

Then suddenly, the sun broke through. I woke up one morning and the cloud was gone. Peace had returned, strength was coming back, and my outlook on the day was positive.

While listening to praise and worship music, the song "Always Good," by Andrew Peterson, came on.[1] Two lines from this song really touched my heart. The first: "He suffered like I never could." I can never go through anything worse than the suffering Jesus faced on the cross on my behalf. The second: "Somehow this sorrow is shaping my heart like it should." Everything I go through God uses to mold and shape me further into the image of His Beloved Son. No experience ever goes to waste.

> *And we know that in all things God works for the good of those who love Him, who have been called according to His purpose (Romans 8:28 NKJV).*

I know there will be another valley in my future, but I also know that He will bring me out as He always does. So, if you are struggling right now, keep walking, keep putting one foot in front of the other. God is going to bring you out the other side. I know how exhausting the journey can be, but it will end. The sun always rises each morning, and it will rise for you.

> *When you pass through the waters, I will be with you; and through the rivers, they shall not overflow you. When you walk through the fire, you shall not be burned, nor shall the flame scorch you (Isaiah 43:2 NKJV).*

26

Letter to Lisa

The Lord is close to the brokenhearted
and saves those who are crushed in spirit.
(Psalm 34:18 NIV)

I wrote this letter to a precious friend who had just lost her brother. In eighteen months, she had faced the loss of her dad due to a car accident, the death of her step-dad as a result of a long-term illness, and then the death of her baby brother who had committed suicide. She gave me permission to put it in this book in the hope it might help someone facing a similar tragedy.

> What do you say to a friend who has lost loved one after loved one? How do you comfort her when it culminates in losing the baby brother she took care of and mothered when they were growing up?
>
> Do I tell her God is still in heaven and still on His throne? He is. Do I tell her He takes care of the broken-hearted and heals them? He does. Do I tell her He aches with her and holds every tear close to His heart? He has her every tear stored in a bottle. Do I tell her she will see her brother again? Yes, she will, without a doubt. Do I tell her her brother fought a disability

bravely for many years and she should be proud of him? I know that she is.

Do I tell her her brother stepped through the door straight into the arms of Jesus? He did. Do I tell her sometimes God heals on the other side of the grave? I don't understand why, but He does. Do I tell her her brother is at peace, no longer in pain, and in the arms of Jesus, and what better place can there be? I can, but that is small comfort to her right now. Do I tell her I understand her pain? I don't. I cannot possibly understand the anguish and heartbreak she is feeling right now.

What I can tell her, during this terrible time, is that she has a spiritual family whom she has never met. Her family in Christ at my church, who prayed for her and continue to pray for her. One of these family members, while sitting in vigil at the bedside of his dying friend, took the time to pray for her, and who, the day after his friend died, had her on the forefront of his mind, and despite his own pain took the time to ask how she was doing. I can remind her she has amazing friends in her life, who showed their love in the outpouring of gifts for her new home. I can remind her of the two beautiful daughters and the son God gave her.

I can tell her she has the kindest, most generous heart of anyone I have ever met. That she took the time to find help for an ill cat whose owner would have been devastated if she had lost her precious pet. That she filled Christmas stockings with gifts she could ill afford to buy to make sure children had a Christmas. That she is the first person to step up whenever anyone is in need and, when friends are going through their own heart-break, she is there with them every step of the way, comforting and encouraging them. I can tell her how much her friendship and loyalty has meant to me, and thank her for the love and care she has shown me during my times of heartache. I can tell her God sees her gentle, humble heart, which is so precious to Him.

And the last thing I can tell her is God loves her so much He would rather die a horrific death on a cross than be in heaven without her. That same God has her in His hands, taking care of her and protecting her. When He died, He looked down through the annals of time and saw her face and said, "It is worth every ounce of pain and every drop of blood to have her as My child."

The hopeless grief will eventually give way to peace. Keep holding on to your friends and most importantly, keep holding on to Him because He is holding you every step of the way.

27

Second-Class Citizens?

*There is neither Jew nor Gentile, neither slave nor free
nor is there male and female, for you are all one in Christ Jesus.
(Galatians 3:28 NIV)*

An issue I am often questioned about is how God views women. A self-proclaimed feminist told me one day that the Bible treated women as second-class citizens. She had not read the Bible but wasn't going to confuse the issue with any facts. Her entire opinion was based on hearsay and what she thought the Bible said.

I pointed out one of the unique features of the Bible is the way it exalts women. Starting in Genesis, God states men and women both bear the stamp of His image, and stories are woven throughout the Bible of women playing prominent roles in Biblical narratives. Pagan religions debased women. Christianity lifted them up. God places women right next to men because both sexes bear His image.

The conversation started with this woman's take on Paul, who she designated as a misogynist. I pointed her to Paul's writing in the verse above where he makes it very clear that we are all one in Christ.

Further proof that Paul had great respect for women, and that women are always uplifted wherever the gospel is preached, is in Acts 16:11-15. These verses describe his travel to Macedonia and how he went to the riverside to talk with the women who customarily met there to pray. The Holy Spirit was already at work preparing the heart of one woman, Lydia, who would become an integral part of Paul's ministry.

Lydia was a successful businesswoman. In Acts 16, she is described as a "seller of purple, of the city of Thyatira." She evidently had a deep hunger for God because she met with other women each day on the banks of the river to talk about the things of God. She became Paul's first European convert and she used her wealth to assist Paul in spreading the gospel. She was generous in her hospitality, opening her home to Christian believers. Paul also refers to women as fellow workers in the Epistles *(Romans 16)*.

Then I gave my feminist friend what I personally believe is the ultimate proof of how God sees women. The pivotal moment in history that changed the world forever, the event the entire concept of Christianity hangs on, is the resurrection, and women were an essential part in the telling of this good news.

When Christ rose from the dead, the first people He appeared to were women. If the apostles had wanted to fabricate the story that Jesus had risen from the dead, the last people they would have used as the first witnesses would have been women. In the Hebrew culture of those days, women were second-class citizens. They were totally subject to their husbands, they were not allowed to give testimony in a court of law, and, in many cases, not treated much better than farm animals. But Jesus trusted the witness of His first appearance to the women. All four gospel writers confirm this.

> *Now after the Sabbath, as the first day of the week began*
> *to dawn, Mary Magdalene and the other Mary came to*
> *see the tomb; So they went out quickly from the tomb with*

fear and great joy, and ran to bring His disciples word (Matthew 28:1; 8 NKJV).

Now when He rose early on the first day of the week, He appeared first to Mary Magdalene, out of whom He had cast seven demons (Mark 16:9 NKJV).

Now on the first day of the week, very early in the morning, they, and certain other women with them, came to the tomb bringing the spices which they had prepared. But they found the stone rolled away from the tomb. Then they went in and did not find the body of the Lord Jesus; Then they returned from the tomb and told all these things to the eleven and to all the rest. It was Mary Magdalene, Joanna, Mary the mother of James, and the other women with them, who told these things to the apostles (Luke 24:1-3; 9-10 NKJV).

Now on the first day of the week Mary Magdalene went to the tomb early, while it was still dark, and saw that the stone had been taken away from the tomb; Now when she had said this, she turned around and saw Jesus standing there, and did not know that it was Jesus. Jesus said to her, "Woman, why are you weeping? Whom are you seeking?" She, supposing Him to be the gardener, said to Him, "Sir, if You have carried Him away, tell me where You have laid Him, and I will take Him away." Jesus said to her, "Mary! (John 20:1; 14-16 NKJV).

This issue of women being second-class citizens came up a second time a few days later. A male co-worker took a mutual friend to church and proceeded to tell her the Bible states women are subject to men. He thought he was safe in saying this because he knew she didn't know much scripture. However, he did not expect her to come pounding into my office to ask for clarity on the subject. With great joy, I not only rolled him under the bus, I personally drove it over him.

I showed her Ephesians 5:22-33 and pointed out the following:

a) It does not say women must submit to ALL men, just to their husbands.

b) Submission does not mean servitude and obeying a husband's every command and whim. It is all about order. God is no respecter of persons, but in matters of role and function He has made distinctions. The best example of role and function is probably the armed forces. Without rank, it would be chaos. A colonel in the army is not necessarily a better person than the private he is commanding, but for the system to work there must be order.

c) The Bible makes clear husbands are to love their wives the way Christ loves His church. If my husband is going to love me and treat me the way Christ loves and treats His church, I am quite happy to be subject to him.

She was delighted with the clarification and marched off to find him. He was hiding under his desk, which I had noticed, but having already thrown him under the bus, I decided to show some mercy and not point this out to the avenging angel searching for him. Although, this should teach him not to mess about with the Word.

28

Why the Wilderness?

You enlarged my path under me, so my feet did not slip.
(Psalm 18:36 NKJV)

Often, we end up in our version of the wilderness—in a situation that we do not understand, and where we can't comprehend what God is doing. He seems to have us on a journey that makes no sense to us with detour after detour.

The Hebrew slaves, led out of Egypt by Moses, were headed to the Promised Land. The obvious route was short, along the coastline to Canaan, but instead God led them through the Red Sea and into the Sinai desert. The coastline route would have taken approximately eleven days. But God knew something they didn't. Between them and the Promised Land were the warring Philistines. The former slaves, fresh out of Egypt and with no knowledge of how to wage war, would have been sitting ducks.

God may have told Moses the reason, but if He did, Moses did not share it with the Hebrews, which led to grumbling and complaining as the long journey continued with obstacle after obstacle and no apparent end in sight.

God also knew His people needed to be trained, taught, and given time to grow in their faith before they would be able to take possession of the Promised Land. He had given them the land, but they still had to occupy the ground. So into the desert they went.

And that is what He often does with us. We must have a "wilderness" experience so we can grow and be strengthened in our faith. Every trial, every moment of pain, every instance of fear and confusion, He uses for our good.

> *And we know that all things work together for good to those who love God, to those who are the called according to His purpose (Romans 8:28 NKJV).*

God continually strengthens our spiritual muscles and prepares us for what He has in store for us so we are able to carry the weight of the blessings coming our way. Sounds counter intuitive that a blessing could be a "weight," doesn't it? But without His teaching, what God has ahead for us could easily become a burden and not a blessing if we are not ready for it.

> *He brought me out into a spacious place; He rescued me because He delighted in me (Psalm 18:19 NIV).*

David wrote this verse after his years of exile had ended and he was now king of Israel. God used those years in the desert when he was running from Saul, hiding in caves, with enemies all around him, as a training ground for his future role as king. He would never have been able to fulfil his calling as king without those times of trouble where all he had to hold onto was his faith in his God.

As you travel through your wilderness, keep clinging to His Hand, knowing it is all in His control. Don't let fear tell you that you have been forgotten. God will never forget you. He is always working on your behalf.

*See, I have engraved you on the palms of my hands; your
walls are ever before me (Isaiah 49:16 NIV).*

Hold onto His Word and keep walking. One day, you will look back and
see the whole picture and thank Him for those difficult times.

"Don't question in the dark what God showed you in
the light" (V. Raymond Edman).

29

Hold onto Hope

May the God of hope fill you with all joy and peace as you trust in Him
so that you may overflow with hope by the power of the Holy Spirit.
(Romans 15:13 NIV)

The Bible instructs us to hope. But how? What do you do when you have reached the point of giving up and just don't have it in you to hope any longer? I always thought I had to somehow dredge this hope up myself.

Reading the scripture above for about the twentieth time, it suddenly dawned on me. The words I was missing were *"by the power of the Holy Spirit."* It's not my job to go digging for hope and then try to hold onto it with bloody fingernails; it is the work of the Holy Spirit. By His power, not mine. Suddenly it became so much easier. Now I pray for the Holy Spirit to fill me with hope, instead of trying to dredge it up and keep it going by sheer willpower.

Trusting Him and holding on to hope, however, can be tortuous, especially when you are praying and waiting and nothing seems to be happening. But always remember, it may seem like He is doing nothing, but under the surface, He is working and moving things into place to fulfil your desires and bring His plan for your life to fulfilment.

The Israelites were facing an ocean on one side and a horde of angry Egyptians on the other. They were rightly terrified, but what they couldn't see was God's hand about to provide a dry path through the water to the other side.

When the next generation arrived at the Jordan River, the priests were instructed to carry the ark and march directly into the river. Joshua told them God would open the river as soon as they stepped into it. Usually the Jordan River is only about a hundred feet wide, but it was at flood stage, which could easily make it a mile wide. It must have taken great faith and an expectant hope to take that first step because they could not see God working upstream stopping the water flow.

Of course, there is a caveat to praying and asking Him for something. Your desires need to be in line with His Word. You can only be sure of your hope if you know it is in alignment with His Word. Remember, too, that His ways are not our ways. You need to trust and believe God knows what is best for you, and that His will always stems from His love.

Sometimes, even though our desires may be in line with His Word, God may still not fulfil them in the way we expect. However, even though He may not always give you what you want in the way you want, you can be sure He will give you His absolute best.

> *"For My thoughts are not your thoughts, nor are your ways*
> *My ways," says the Lord. "For as the heavens are higher*
> *than the earth, so are My ways higher than your ways, and*
> *My thoughts than your thoughts" (Isaiah 55:8-9 NKJV).*

Ask God to clarify your desires and then rest in His goodness.

> *Delight yourself also in the Lord, and He shall give you*
> *the desires of your heart (Psalm 37:4 NKJV).*

"No other religion, no other, promises new bodies, hearts, and minds. Only in the gospel of Christ do hurting people find such incredible hope" (Joni Eareckson Tada).

30

When Hope Runs Dry

How long, O Lord, will I call for help,
And You will not hear?
(Habakkuk 1:2 NASB)

Ever been here? Tired, weary, out of hope, tired of holding on. Friends are super helpful telling you to stand, have faith, sit, be still, keep going, the joy of the Lord is your strength. And sometimes you just want to smack them for this. You don't want to hope any longer because it's better to have no hope than constantly feel like your hope is being dashed as you wait and trust while nothing happens.

David understood that feeling.

My heart is stricken and withered like grass,
So that I forget to eat my bread.
Because of the sound of my groaning
My bones cling to my skin.
I am like a pelican of the wilderness;
I am like an owl of the desert.
I lie awake,
And am like a sparrow alone on the housetop.
(Psalm 102:4-7 NKJV)

I wasn't sure if pelicans did live in the wilderness of Judea but, apparently, they do, at least for a short while. Great White pelicans use the lakes in Israel as a watering stop on their migratory path to Africa.

> *The Lord will guide you continually, and satisfy your soul in drought, and strengthen your bones; you shall be like a watered garden, and like a spring of water, whose waters do not fail (Isaiah 58:11 NKJV).*

The Lord brought David through just as He will bring you through. He will strengthen your bones, give you fresh water along the way, and guide you safely to your destination. You will make it to your version of Africa. Just hold onto His Word.

31

He Came for the Outcasts

When Jesus heard it, He said to them, "Those who are well have no need of a physician, but those who are sick.
I did not come to call the righteous, but sinners, to repentance."
(Mark 2:17 NKJV)

Jesus came for the outcasts, not for the squeaky clean "religious" people who believed they had no need for a Savior. The tone of His ministry was set by the first three miracles He did for those then regarded as being on the lowest rung of the social ladder.

The first miracle was a leper, the ultimate outcast in society.

> *And behold, a leper came and worshipped Him saying, "Lord, if You are willing, You can make me clean." Then Jesus put out His hand and touched him saying, "I am willing, be cleansed." Immediately, his leprosy was cleansed (Matthew 8:3-4 NKJV).*

Jesus "touched" him. It was probably the first time the man had experienced a human touch in years. When his leprosy had come upon him, he would have had to leave his home and his loved ones to live a lonely, love-starved existence with death as the only possible release.

The next miracle was for a centurion, requesting help for his desperately sick servant. Not only was this man a Gentile, but as a Roman soldier he was part of the hated Roman occupation.

> *Now when Jesus had entered Capernaum, a centurion came to Him, pleading with Him, saying, "Lord, my servant is lying at home paralyzed, dreadfully tormented." And Jesus said to him, "I will come and heal him" (Matthew 8:5-7 NKJV).*

The third miracle was for Peter's mother-in-law. In the Hebrew culture of those days, women were regarded as second-class citizens. They were totally subject to their husbands and were not allowed to give witness in a court of law. Often, they were regarded on the same level as farm animals. (Side note: if you want to know how Jesus views women, read the gospels and see who He appeared to first and trusted with the news of His resurrection.)

> *Now when Jesus had come into Peter's house, He saw his wife's mother lying sick with fever. So He touched her hand, and the fever left her (Matthew 8:14-15 NKJV).*

The list of Jesus serving the outcasts goes on and on. He healed the woman with a hemorrhagic issue. For this woman, there was virtually nothing that could have been worse than her situation. Having a perpetual flow of blood would have made her unclean. She would not have been allowed to touch her husband or her children. Anything she touched would have been considered unclean, so she would not even have been able to take care of her home. She would have been socially ostracized and left to a lonely existence. The physical load must also have been unbearable, constant exhaustion and the endless rounds of supposed cures. She reached out to Jesus, and He to her.

For she said, "If only I may teach His clothes, I shall be made well"…. And He said to her, "Daughter, your faith has made you sell. Go in peace and be healed from your affliction" (Mark 5:28, 34 NKJV).

If you feel like an outcast, and wonder if He has time for you, He does. He came for people like you. Reach out to Him and you will feel His loving touch.

32

Lazarus

He cried with a loud voice, Lazarus, come forth!
(John 11:43 NKJV)

Mary and Martha were devastated by the loss of Lazarus. They knew Jesus could have healed their brother. They had seen Him heal the sick and open the eyes of the blind. But in their view, He had not arrived in time to do any good. Their brother was dead. They had sent word to Jesus that His friend was sick, but instead of coming right away, Jesus tarried.

Jesus had a good reason for this given the belief of the time. The Jews believed the soul hovered around the body for three days hoping to re-enter it. On the fourth day, after noticing the body was decomposing, the soul would depart. Only then was death considered irreversible.[1] Lazarus had already been dead four days when Jesus arrived. At this point, the Jews present at the grave site would know that only a divine miracle could raise Lazarus to life.

What Mary and Martha were viewing as a failure, God was seeing as the chance for a greater purpose and a greater miracle. The raising of Lazarus would vividly demonstrate His power over death to all those present.

Jesus said to her, "I am the resurrection and the life. He who believes in Me, though he may die, he shall live" (John 11:25 NKJV).

Sometimes when we are walking in a sea of pain and confusion, we do not understand what God is doing. But often He has a far better plan. We are seeing one frame in the film of our life. He sees the full picture. Trust Him even when the circumstances look dark and defeat seems inevitable. Don't ask why? Ask what? What, God, do you want me to learn through this experience? What do you want me to do in this experience? The goal in every situation is that Jesus and the Father be glorified. Remember, God's plan for you comes from His heart of love. He will always do what is best for you.

Keep walking, keep believing. For all you know, you could be minutes away from your resurrection.

33

Stir Up Your Gift

Therefore, I remind you to stir up the gift of God which is in you.
(2 Timothy 1:6 NKJV)

But each of you has your own gift from God; one has this gift,
another has that.
(1 Corinthians 7:7 NKJV)

I am not creative. I cannot draw, I cannot paint, and I definitely cannot sing (well, not in tune anyway). This is not false modesty. The creative genes in my family bypassed me. I'm not quite sure where they went, but they did not come down to me.

I am still scarred by my mother congratulating me on the beautiful cow I drew for her when I was a child. It was a horse. And the bunny I drew looked like an amoeba with ears. My friend, Jennifer, and I were asked very politely by our teacher if we could just mime when the class sang.

However, I did a great drawing on my whiteboard of Oswald, the ostrich. My-co-workers were deeply impressed by my talent. A friend cottoned on right away and asked when had I taken to art forgery?

So, I have gone through life believing I do not have a gift. But Paul says we all do. *"Stir up the gift of God which is in you."* Therefore, it followed I had to have a gift of some sort. I just needed to find it.

When we think gifts, we immediately think gifts of the Holy Spirit (1 Corinthians 12:4-11) – wisdom, prophecy, knowledge, and so on. But there are others. What of compassion? Kindness? The willingness to listen and just be there for the hurting? Patience? Encouragement? Barnabas, who accompanied Paul on Paul's missionary journeys was known as the "son of encouragement." After Paul's conversion, it was Barnabas who stood up for Paul and assured the Jerusalem church that Paul was truly converted. Understandably, they were suspicious of Paul whose reputation as a persecutor of the church was well known.

> *And Joses, who was also named Barnabas by the apostles (which is translated Son of Encouragement), a Levite of the country of Cyprus (Acts 4:36 NKJV).*

You are unique. God made only one of you, and He had the plan for your life in place long before you were born. *"Before I formed you in the womb I knew you, before you were born I set you apart" (Jeremiah 1:5 NIV).* Therefore, it follows He has placed the gift(s) in you that will be needed to fulfil that plan.

> *I praise you because I am fearfully and wonderfully made (Psalm 139:14 NKJV).*

If you have any doubt that you are not "fearfully and wonderfully" made, just stop and ponder your DNA. Starting with just four characters, your three billion-character DNA is formed. If you took the DNA out of one cell and stretched it out, it would be six feet long. To read your DNA, reading one character per second, night and day, would take ninety-six years.[1]

All gifts are equally powerful, but all are different. As you get to know Christ deeper and deeper, your gift will become apparent.

*As each one has received a gift, minister it to one another,
as good stewards of the manifold grace of God (1 Peter
4:10 NKJV).*

I have since been told my gift is encouragement, which has been confirmed by others. One of these people even looked at me and said, "Duh,
you didn't realize that?" I am thrilled with my gift. I am in great company with Barnabas, "the son of encouragement."

Seek and embrace your gifts too.

34

In the Crucible

But he knows the way that I take;
When he has tested me, I will come forth as gold.
(Job 23:10 NKJV)

For you, O God, have tested us; you have refined us as silver is refined.
(Psalm 66:10 NKJV)

I will refine them like silver and test them like gold.
(Zechariah 13:9 NIV)

In the crucible—the toughest place to be.[1] It's a time of testing. It's hard. It's painful. It sometimes feels never-ending. But God knows the plan He has for your life, and He knows what trials and heartaches are going to come your way. So He prepares you for them, and sometimes it is in the crucible.

Consider it a privilege. It means God believes you are worth molding and shaping. It means He has a greater purpose for your life that He is preparing you for.

> *My son do not despise the chastening of the Lord, nor detest His correction; For whom the Lord loves He corrects, just as a father the son in whom he delights (Proverbs 3:11-12 NKJV).*

The metalworker heats the metal in his crucible until it becomes liquid and the impurities (dross) bubble up to the surface. He then skims it off and boils the metal, again and again, constantly scooping the dross off the top until the moment the metal is pure and he can see his reflection in it. God does the same with us. He boils us again and again, skimming the impurities off the surface until His image is reflected in us.

> *These trials will show that your faith is genuine. It is being tested as fire tests and purifies gold – though your faith is far more precious than mere gold (1 Peter 1:7 NLT).*

John Rippon in his hymn, "How Firm a Foundation", pens it beautifully:

> *When through fiery trials, thy pathways shall lie,*
> *My grace, all sufficient, shall be thy supply;*
> *The flame shall not hurt thee, I only design*
> *Thy dross to consume, and thy gold to refine.*

Elijah was in the crucible at Zarephath. The word Zarephath comes from the Hebrew word that means "to melt" or "to smelt." Zarephath was a place of refinement, a place of purification by fire, for Elijah.

After Elijah called out King Ahab and Queen Jezebel for their wicked, idolatrous ways, God hid Elijah by a brook at Cherith to protect him from the vengeful king and queen. During that time, God provided a fresh spring of water for Elijah to drink from and ravens to airlift food to him. But then it came time for the life of comparative ease to end and for Elijah to be tested further. So God sent him into the crucible at Zarephath. God knew what He had planned for Elijah, and it was going to require great strength and faith. The first test he faced was potential starvation when he discovered the widow God had told him to go to was in dire straits herself. He had to trust God to keep the small amount of oil and flour remaining in her pantry flowing as long as was needed.

That was only the first test, more followed. But at the end of it all, Elijah came out stronger than before and ready to face his biggest challenge yet—the Baal priests at Mount Carmel.

Elijah may have avoided death and gone to heaven in a chariot of fire, but according to James, *"Elijah was just as human as we are (James 5:17 CEB).* He faced the same trials and disappointments we do, and had to undergo the same testing and trying by God.

The Lord also tested Joseph when he was sold as a slave, taken to Egypt, and forced to endure two years in prison. God knew exactly what Joseph was going to need when he became second-in-command in Egypt, and He prepared him for the task ahead with all that came before it. It was through Joseph that many lives were saved in the time of famine.

> *He sent a man before them—Joseph—who was sold as a slave. They hurt his feet with fetters, he was laid in irons. Until the time that his word came to pass, the word of the Lord tested him (Psalm 105:17-19 NKJV).*

Unfortunately, trials are not optional. God has not promised a life without trials. Suffering serves an important purpose in our lives; He uses it to shape us into His image.

> *Behold, I have refined you, but not as silver; I have tested you in the furnace of affliction (Isaiah 48:10 NKJV).*

The one thing to hold on to, while you are in the smelting pot, is that, just as God was in the fire with Meshach, Shadrach and Abednego, He is also in the fire with you. Warren Wiersbe said it beautifully, "When God permits His children to go through the furnace, He keeps His eye on the clock and His hand on the thermostat. His loving heart knows how much and how long."

God will not leave you in the crucible one minute longer than is necessary. And when you emerge, you will be tested and refined, and on the path to becoming pure gold.

35

Under the Shadow of His Wings

He will cover you with His feathers and under His wings
you will find refuge.
(Psalm 91:4 NIV)

P salm 91 is a psalm about a battle, but amid the tumult and chaos, David still felt the protection of His Lord. He knew beyond a shadow of a doubt he was protected under the wings of God. David called His protector my Rock, my Fortress, my Strong Tower. We call him Jesus.

I had a front row seat this summer of how a mother bird takes care of her little ones. A wren had made her nest in a hanging basket on my patio. Neither rain nor shine, nor heat nor cold, could force her from her nest and the three babies sheltering under her wings. Not even a thunderstorm could dislodge her. She just hunkered down and kept her babies warm and dry underneath her body. She was ready to defend them to the death had any predator dared to attack them. A small wren can suddenly become a raging momma bear if she thinks her children are in danger.

Jesus does the same for us. Anyone or anything that tries to harm us must go through Him first. When the soldiers came for Him in the garden of Gethsemane, He stepped between them and His disciples, telling the soldiers to let the disciples go, that He was the one they were looking for. Hell was going to have to go through Him to get to His children.

Jesus said to them, "I am He." And Judas, who betrayed Him, also stood with them. Now when He said to them, "I am He," they drew back and fell to the ground. Then He asked them again, "Whom are you seeking?" And they said, "Jesus of Nazareth." Jesus answered, "I have told you that I am He. Therefore, if you seek Me, let these go their way," that the saying might be fulfilled which He spoke, "Of those whom You gave Me I have lost none" (John 18:5-9 NKJV).

When I was a child, I had my own small version of being under the shadow of His wings. After my Dad died, life became difficult and I needed an escape. In the afternoons, after homework was done, I would grab my dogs and head into the sanctuary of our back garden. It was wild and overgrown, perfect for an adventurous child. Sometimes I was not in the mood for adventure, however, and just wanted a safe place to hide. My favorite spot was under a massive lilac bush. I discovered a hollowed-out section, just big enough for me and my dogs to shelter. I would lie under the canopy of branches, the sweet smell of lilac permeating the air, sunlight dappling the leaves, the dogs gently snoring, and bees bumbling and buzzing. I felt safe and protected in my cocoon.

This is how I think a baby bird feels when it is warm and safe under the downy body of its mom. And that is how I picture His wings over me. They also have the sweet aroma of lilac.

Whenever you are afraid, remind yourself of His wings covering you. Nestle down into the warmth and comfort of His care and listen to the beating of His heart. You are safe, secure, and protected, and nothing can get to you to harm you.

36

No Condemnation

When Jesus had raised Himself up and saw no one but the woman,
He said to her, 'Woman, where are those accusers of yours?
Has no one condemned you?'
She said, 'No one, Lord.' And Jesus said to her,
'Neither do I condemn you; go and sin no more.'
(John 8:10-11 NKJV)

When you fall, when you make a major mistake, when you realize you have failed miserably, it can be overwhelming. You may wonder how God can ever forgive you. Satan cleverly built and baited the trap, covered it with twigs and branches; you didn't recognize the set up and you blundered right into it. Now you're at the bottom of a pit, hurt, bruised, and bleeding, and the guilt comes in shattering waves. All you can think is Jesus died for you, that the pain and anguish He went through on the cross was for you, and you let Him down.

Take comfort from the woman caught in adultery in the verse above. Dragged into the court of public opinion by a bunch of self-righteous Pharisees, terrified and panicking, she desperately looked around her for someone who would step up and protect her. She found that Someone. Thrown down at His feet, she looked up into the only eyes that were full of kindness and love.

Unlike the Pharisees, Jesus didn't see an object to be used as a lesson to others. Instead, He saw His daughter, scarred and weary from sin, but still His daughter—the same child He formed in the womb, the same child He knew before time began, and the same child He was going to go to the cross and die for.

> *There is therefore now no condemnation to those who are in Christ Jesus, who do not walk according to the flesh, but according to the Spirit (Romans 8:1 NKJV).*

Paul, probably more than any other apostle, understood forgiveness. When his story began, he was a fire-breathing zealot dragging Christians off to be killed. He even held the coats of the murderers stoning Stephen. But God reached out to him and Paul became God's apostle to the Gentiles. If anyone experienced God's grace, it was Paul.

> *No, dear brothers and sisters, I have not achieved it, but I focus on this one thing: Forgetting the past and looking forward to what lies ahead, I press on to reach the end of the race and receive the heavenly prize for which God, through Christ Jesus, is calling us (Philippians 3:13-14 NLT).*

When you trip and fall, get up and run straight to Him. Look into His eyes of love, ask Him to forgive you, and then move on. It's over, under the blood of Christ. God says very clearly that He does not remember your sin. Follow His example and do the same.

> *I, even I, am he who blots out your transgressions, for my own sake, and remembers your sins no more (Isaiah 43:25 NIV).*

> *For I will be merciful and gracious toward their sins and I will remember their deeds of unrighteousness no more (Hebrews 8:12 AMPC).*

As far as the east is from the west, so far has He removed our transgressions from us (Psalm 103:12 NIV).

Do you know how far east is from west? It's immeasurable. It's infinite and never-ending. If you go north or south, eventually you will reach a stopping point and have to change direction. But going east and west you just keep going and going and going, much like the Energizer Bunny. There is no ending. That is how God views your sins. They are so far away from you the distance cannot be measured. They are gone, erased by the power of the cross.

By the way, the Pharisees are still alive and well today. They are now in the form of self-righteous religious people who are happier to parade someone's sin than to love and restore the person. Don't allow them to put you under condemnation.

37

His Will is His Love

For I know the thoughts that I think toward you, says the Lord,
thoughts of peace and not of evil, to give you a future and a hope.
(Jeremiah 29:11 NKJV)

When I read the comment "His will is His love," I had an "aha" moment. I, like many people, viewed God's will as something that would be incredibly hard to do and, more than likely, be extremely unpleasant, such as being sent to be a missionary in a remote, terrifying place populated with man-eating plants and bugs the size of pterodactyls.

However, once the truth dawned on me that His will is always underpinned by His immeasurable, all-encompassing love, my perception totally changed. I began not to fear, but to instead feel excitement and anticipation for what He has planned for me.

God is my loving, heavenly Father so no matter what His plans are for me, they will come from His heart of love. Jesus, who is *"the express image of His person" (Hebrews 1:3)*, said:

> *If a son asks for bread from any father among you, will he give him a stone? Or if he asks for a fish, will he give him a serpent instead of a fish? Or if he asks for an egg, will he offer him a scorpion? If you then, being evil, know how to give good gifts to your children, how much more will*

your heavenly Father give the Holy Spirit to those who ask Him! (Luke 11:11-13 NKJV).

God even uses all our mistakes, trials, struggles, and heartache to skillfully weave the beautiful fabric of our lives.

And we know that all things work together for good to those who love God, to those who are the called according to His purpose (Romans 8:28 NKJV).

We don't need to walk in fear of His will. It will always be the absolute best for us. Of that there is no doubt.

38

Gentle as the Dew

Let My teaching fall like rain,
And My words descend like dew.
Like showers on new grass,
Like abundant rain on tender plants.
(Deuteronomy 32:2 NIV)

This morning I took my dogs for their usual walk. The sun was just coming up. The air was crisp and clean. The dew was sparkling on the grass. Later, during my quiet time, I came across this scripture, *"your strength will be renewed each day like the morning dew"* (Psalm 110:3 NLT). It was a word sent in perfect time because I was dragging myself around trying to build some energy to face the day.

In the Bible, dew is seen as a blessing. Dew is silent and humble. Unlike rain, it does not draw attention to itself. Dew never causes damage. It is a beautiful likeness of Jesus—humble, gentle, nourishing, and coming down from above.

> *When the dew settled on the camp at night, the manna*
> *also came down (Numbers 11:9 NIV).*

God sent the dew along with the manna each night to sustain the children of Israel in the wilderness. Dew was a nightly reminder of God's care.

Dew is vital to the existence of Israel. It does not rain from April to October, and all vegetation would die if it were not for the dew. Rain is needed in the winter season for the grass and early crops to grow. Dew is needed in the summer for the later crops and fruit to grow.

The dew is amazingly abundant in Israel thanks to the proximity of the country to the Mediterranean Sea, which allows vast amounts of moisture to be soaked up into the atmosphere. Gideon wrung out a full bowel of water from the fleece he had put out overnight because it was so full of dew. (God had called Gideon to be a judge and a deliverer of His people. Gideon needed reassurance that it was indeed God who was speaking to him, so he asked for a sign in the form of a fleece. The Lord graciously made the fleece wet at Gideon's request as proof it was Him calling Gideon to service.)

> *And it was so. When he arose early the next morning and squeezed the fleece, he drained the dew from the fleece, a bowl full of water (Judges 6:38 NASB).*

Like the dew, God's Word soaks us and nourishes us. It help us grow and flourish. It is as essential to our life as water.

> *The Lord by wisdom founded the earth, by understanding He established the heavens. By His knowledge the deeps were broken up and the skies drip with dew (Proverbs 3:19-20 NASB).*

> *I will be to Israel like a refreshing dew from heaven. Israel will blossom like the lily; it will send roots deep into the soil like the cedars in Lebanon. Its branches will spread out like beautiful olive trees, as fragrant as the cedars of Lebanon (Hosea 14:5-6 NLT).*

Let His heavenly dew settle down into your soul, soak yourself in His Word and be refreshed.

39

Age is No Impediment

You are never too old to set a new goal or dream a new dream
- C.S. Lewis

I am aging. I don't like to admit it, but I am. I now receive regular membership offers from AARP, which I find very annoying. More seriously, I often wonder if God has any more work for me to do and if He can still use me. However, my Bible shows me God can, and will, use us, no matter what our age. All He needs is a willing heart.

Abraham thought he was too old. Jeremiah thought he was too young. Timothy thought he was too inexperienced. Noah was past his prime. God disagreed with all of them.

> *Then Abraham fell on his face and laughed, and said in his heart, "shall a child be born to a man who is one hundred years old? And shall Sarah, who is ninety years old, bear a child?" (Genesis 17:17 NKJV).*

> *Then said I: "Ah, Lord God! Behold, I cannot speak, for I am a youth" (Jeremiah 1:6 NKJV).*

> *Let no one despise your youth, but be an example to the believers in word, in conduct, in love, in spirit, in faith, in purity (1 Timothy 4:12 NKJV).*

Moses thought life had passed him by. He had left the courts of Pharaoh for a simple life in the wilderness herding sheep. He was eighty when the call from God came. One would think a forty-year-old Moses would have been a better bet for leading a few million Hebrews on what would ultimately become a forty-year hike in the wilderness. But God knew He needed a wiser, older, more tempered Moses to fulfil His calling. And speaking of temper, He also needed a Moses who had learned to control his. Murdering Egyptians whenever they irked him would not have been helpful to the cause. Also, what Moses learned in those years in the desert tending his sheep was perfect for handling the stubborn, hard-headed Hebrew flock he was going to be leading and his survival skills and understanding of the desert would be invaluable for the long march ahead under the harsh conditions.

Jeremiah was called when he was a youth and was horrified at the prospect. Self-confidence was not his strongest attribute, and God had to strengthen and encourage him that he could do whatever God called him to do.

> But the Lord said to me, "Don't say, 'I am only a boy.' You must go everywhere I send you, and you must say everything I tell you to say. Don't be afraid of anyone, because I am with you to protect you," says the Lord (Jeremiah 1:7-8 NCV).

Timothy was young and insecure. He was dealing with people older than himself in the church at Ephesus. Paul had to encourage him in the verse above not to let anyone make him feel that he was not capable of handling the job he had been called to do.

Noah was a hundred years old when God called him to service. And not just any service, service that required hard manual labor. It must have taken tremendous faith for Noah to take that first swipe of his axe to the gopherwood tree. Can you imagine being told by God to build an ark?

Noah had never seen rain, never mind a flood. In antediluvian times, the earth was a biosphere and a canopy of moisture covered the earth keeping the land watered.[1] Added to that, the people of Noah's time also had never experienced rain, so the mocking must have been intense. "Oh dear, Noah is still at it building his wooden contraption. There will be no gopherwood trees left at the rate he is going!"

Someone once said that those God calls, God endows. And He does. He uses the weak, the young, the old, and the foolish to advance His kingdom.

> *But God has chosen the foolish things of the world to put to shame the wise, and God has chosen the weak things of the world to put to shame the things which are mighty (1 Corinthians 1:27 NKJV).*

Age is no impediment, whether you are young or more advanced in years. I always remind myself God is pretty old Himself.

> *Those who are planted in the house of the Lord shall flourish in the courts of our God. They shall still bear fruit in old age; they shall be fresh and flourishing, to declare that the Lord is upright; He is my rock, and there is no unrighteousness in Him (Psalm 92:13-15 NKJV).*

If you think you are too young or too old, think again. Open your heart and let Him show you what amazing adventures He has ahead for you if you are willing to heed His call.

"Don't let age – whether the lack of years or the lack of years remaining – keep you from serving God. The heart for God knows no age" (David Jeremiah).

40

Amazing Grace

For it is by grace you have been saved, through faith, and this is not from
yourselves, it is the gift of God, not by works, so that no one can boast.
(Ephesians 2:8-9 NIV)

We are saved by grace alone, through faith alone, in Christ alone, as
taught by the scriptures alone, for the glory of God alone.

Grace. One word. Five letters. So simple. So amazing. And sometimes
difficult to comprehend. However, three stories demonstrate the incredible grace of God.

The first one is summed up in two words, "and Peter." When the angel
in Jesus' tomb told the women their Lord had risen, He told them to go
tell His disciples and then added two simple words, "and Peter."

> *But go, tell his disciples and Peter, 'He is going ahead of*
> *you into Galilee.' There you will see him, just as he told*
> *you (Mark 16:7 NIV).*

After Peter's betrayal, Jesus made sure that His broken disciple knew he
was forgiven and that he could return to his Lord. Amazing grace.

The second example is "a Pharisee of Pharisees," who had the blood of
countless Christians on his hands. Then he met Christ in a head-on

collision on the road to Damascus. Paul ended up writing two-thirds of the New Testament.

The third person to benefit from God's grace was a slave trader who met Christ in a sinking vessel on a stormy ocean. At the age of twenty-one, John Newton was working on a slave ship, the *Greyhound*, crossing the Atlantic. A violent storm broke out and the ship was swamped. After a long night of frantically pumping water, Newton realized death was almost certain. He pleaded with God to have mercy and, miraculously, both the ship and the crew survived. John Newton wrote the hymn, "Amazing Grace."

So, if you ever think the mistakes and sins in your life preclude you from reaching out to Christ, just remember these two words, "and Peter."

41

Stop Gnawing the Bone

Be still and know that I am God.
(Psalm 46:10 NKJV)

It had been one of those weeks when it felt like my brain was actively trying to kill me. Problems kept resurfacing and I kept stewing over them. By the time Friday came, I was irritated and exhausted. A friend once told me I think too much. He is 100% right; I do. I turn things over and over in my mind, trying to work out a logical solution or a better way to handle the problem.

Many times friends have told me to "let go and let God." So I did, for about two minutes. Then I got concerned maybe God was busy and didn't have time, so I helpfully took back my worries and gnawed them again.

Friday was a day off for me that week, so I told God this time I really was going to hand everything over to Him. I was going to spend the morning in peace and solitude, listening for His voice. (Here is a word of advice: don't tell God you're going to do that unless you are ready to hear from Him.)

I reached for His Word. The first scripture I landed on was, *"words kill, words give life; they're either poison or fruit – you choose"* (Proverbs 18:21 MSG). Ouch! The message was clear. Stop with the negative thoughts.

The next scripture was, *"be still and know that I am God"* (*Psalm 46:10 NKJV*). That was telling me to stop thrashing around and beating myself over the head. A theme was starting to emerge.

Then I landed in Numbers 13 where the spies were reporting back to Moses what they saw in the Promised Land. Ten men came back with negative reports. Only Joshua and Caleb came back with a positive report.

> *"Then Caleb silenced the people before Moses, and said, 'We should go up and take possession of the land, for we can certainly do it'"* (*Numbers 13:30 NIV*).

Guess who were the only two that got to enter the Promised Land.

Here is my takeaway and life lesson learned. When struggling with problems that keeping playing over and over in your head, quiet yourself before the Lord. Just be still for a while. Stop speaking and thinking negatively about the situation (yes, this will be hard to do and those negative thoughts will rise again, but squash them by going back to God's Word). Peace will come to your heart; your pulse rate will return to normal, and you will be able to breathe.

This doesn't mean you won't repeat this pattern of behavior. I have no doubt I will gnaw the bone again in the future. However, having been metaphorically slapped upside the head by the Holy Spirit, I will stop, re-read this passage, and apply the lesson I've learned.

As I was writing this, I had a visual of my problem right in front of me. My dog was gnawing on a rawhide bone she had been dragging out day after day. Despite it now being totally revolting, she won't let it go. I got the message.

42

Stormy Seas

Then He arose and rebuked the wind, and said to the sea,
'Peace, be still!' And the wind ceased and there was a great calm.
(Mark 4:39 NKJV)

I have been through times where I have felt like I have been washed overboard in a shipwreck during a raging storm, clinging desperately to a piece of flotsam, waves washing over my head, choking and spluttering, saltwater burning my nose, just trying to hang on and wondering how long I can hold out. Then a pair of nail-pierced Hands reach out through the spray to grab mine. I know I am now safe, and all is well. Those hands are never going to let me go, though the storm may continue to rage around me. I am anchored, and He will hold me until the chaos subsides and the sun breaks through. Then He will pull me safely to shore and prepare breakfast. It's time to rest.

Storms never bother Him. In the Bible, whenever one blew up, He simply instructed it to stop. He is in charge. He is the King of Kings and the Lord of Lords. The elements have to obey Him because they are part of His creation. He has dominion over all things.

> *For by Him all things were created that are in heaven and*
> *that are on earth, visible and invisible, whether thrones*
> *or dominions or principalities or powers. All things were*
> *created through Him and for Him. And He is before*

all things, and in Him all things consist (Colossians 1:16-17 NKJV).

God never lets any experience in our lives go to waste. While He is guiding you through the storm, He will be teaching and training you to build up your spiritual muscles. A smooth sea never made a skilled sailor.

It's His job to calm the storm; it's your job to hold on.

43

Don't Carry Your Burdens Alone

Come to Me, all you who labor and are heavy laden,
and I will give you rest.
Take My yoke upon you and learn from Me,
for I am gentle and lowly in heart, and your will find rest for your souls.
For My yoke is easy and My burden is light.
(Matthew 11:28-30 NKJV)

I come from a line of Scots and English. The English invented the term "stiff upper lip." This means no matter what happens, you soldier on. No crying, no whining, no bleating. My mother was the epitome of that. I only saw her cry once in my life and that was in frustration and concern over a dog that was traveling home to its parents and got stuck overnight at the airport. I never saw her tears around the death of my dad, uncle, or grandmother. (I know someone is going to ask this—the dog made it safely home without any drama or stress. A kind airport employee took it home for the night and saw it safely onto its flight the next day.)

So, thanks to my heritage, I don't like admitting I am struggling or going through a tough time. I try to soldier on and not let anyone know. One Sunday in church, however, God gave me a much-needed lesson in bearing one another's burdens.

A young woman sitting next to me and my friend cried through the entire service. We passed a note to her asking her to write down what was causing her so much pain so we could pray for her. Glancing down at what she was writing, one word jumped out at me: "immigration." She was currently going through the immigration process and was lonely and scared. There was no future for her in her country of birth; the U.S. was her only hope. After the service concluded, I leaned over and spoke to her. Her face lit up as soon as she heard my accent. God, in His amazing grace, had placed someone next to her who had been through a similar experience and could understand her burden and identify with her.

A couple of weeks later, she came running up to me and threw her arms around me, full of smiles to tell me how much better she was doing, how God was working in her situation, and how finding someone who had also walked the road she was currently trudging along had brought her so much comfort and hope.

It was a huge lesson for me. God means us to help each other and be there for each other. Asking for help and admitting perceived weakness is frightening, but there is a difference in having a burden and being a burden. We often don't reach out for help for fear of being a burden. But there will be times in life when things we are dealing with become just too much to handle alone. God tells us He will bear our burdens, and He does, but He also uses people as His instruments to assist in carrying those burdens. He did not mean any of us to deal with life alone. By allowing people into your life and trusting them, you are not only affirming their value to you, you also open them up to receive the blessings God wants to bestow on them for helping you.

> *Bear one another's burdens, and so fulfil the law of Christ"*
> *(Galatians 6:2 NKJV).*

Don't try to go it alone; reach out and let people help you when you are struggling.

Cast your burden on the Lord, and He shall sustain you; He shall never permit the righteous to be moved (Psalm 55:22 NKJV).

44

God Uses Donkeys

Then the Lord opened the donkey's mouth.
(Numbers 22:28 NKJV)

Something I struggled with for many years, and especially when I worked for a church, was seeing supposed Christians behaving in extremely "unchristian" ways. How could God use people like that? Because people were saved, people were healed, and people were touched by God through their ministry.

A pastor explained to me that God will use anyone who is available. He sees the faith and needs of the person reaching out to Him and meets that faith and need. The person on the stage is simply His vessel.

The story of Balaam and the donkey is a great example of God using whatever and whoever is available to fulfil His purpose.

Balaam was a pagan prophet who was ordered by King Balak of the Moabites to curse the Israelites. Balaam initially refused, after he had a vision in the night from God telling him not to obey the king's orders. But when a second set of messengers came from the king, Balaam agreed to go with them. God knew Balaam's rebellious heart, so He gave Balaam's donkey the ability to speak to Balaam. This miraculous sign opened Balaam's eyes and he obeyed God's instructions not to curse the Israelites.

The prophet's disobedience was no problem to God. He used an equine to accomplish His purpose.

God can, and will, use anyone and anything to bring Christ to the world, be it a blazing light from heaven on a Damascus road as Paul experienced or an aside comment thrown out by an atheist as occurred with C.S. Lewis.

The next time you are wondering how God can use a certain person, first remember no-one is perfect, second remember God reaches out to the lost in whatever way He can, and third, He uses donkeys.

Notice I said donkeys not asses. I was intentionally careful with my nomenclature!

45

The God of the Second Chance

For My thoughts are not your thoughts, nor are your ways My ways,
says the Lord.
For as the heavens are higher than the earth, so are My ways higher than
your ways, and
My thoughts than your thoughts.
(Isaiah 55:8-9 NKJV)

Y ou messed up, you genuinely thought you heard from God, but you were wrong. You did it with a faithful heart, and you truly wanted to obey Him, but you missed it. Or maybe you did hear from God and you did follow what He asked you to do, but it didn't have the outcome you thought it would.

The time will come for you to try again. Joshua had to try again. After the amazing victory at Jericho, along came Ai. Even the word sounds defeatist, "Oh Ai." Ai was a city in Canaan. After Jericho, it was the next place that had to be conquered to allow the Israelites to continue on the path to take the Promised Land. God had clearly instructed the Israelites not to take any plunder from Jericho when the city fell, and He further warned that if they disobeyed Him disaster would come upon them.

Do not take any of the things set apart for destruction, or
you yourselves will be completely destroyed, and you will

bring trouble on the camp of Israel. Everything made from silver, gold, bronze, or iron is sacred to the Lord and must be brought into his treasury (Joshua 6:18-19).

Made overconfident by the victory at Jericho, Joshua did not consult God and sallied forth to attack Ai, unaware that a member of the camp, Achan, had disobeyed God and taken plunder from Jericho.

The result was a crushing defeat and the deaths of twenty-six Israelites. However, the second time Joshua and his men went to Ai, they were victors because, this time, they sought God and followed His counsel. When you follow God's strategy, you win the victory.

Not by might nor by power but by my Spirit says the Lord (Zechariah 4:6 NKJV).

Jonah experienced a second chance as well. But first, he had to go through three days sitting in a whale's belly surrounded by gastric juices, dead fish, and seaweed. Then God gave him a second chance and the whale spewed Jonah out onto the shore. It occurs to me that there were two exits out of the whale. God is His infinite mercy chose the front end.

Peter also knew what it felt like to try again. After a night's fruitless fishing that left him tired, smelly, and ready for sleep, he didn't have a problem with letting Christ sit in his boat to teach the masses on the beach. But when Jesus told him to put out into the water and let his nets down again, in the middle of the day (everyone knows you don't catch fish in the middle of the day), he was less than happy. He obeyed though and the result was the biggest catch of fish he had ever had. He ended up face down in the boat at Jesus' feet.

> *But when Simon Peter saw that, he fell down at Jesus' feet,*
> *saying, "Go away from me Lord, for I am a sinful man!"*
> *(Luke 5:8 NASB).*

This was just a small precursor to one of the greatest second chances in the history of mankind. After denying His Lord three times, heartbroken and in anguish, Peter went back to the only life he knew before meeting Christ—fishing. Even if the story the women at Jesus' tomb had told him was true, that Christ had indeed risen from the dead, what difference would that make to Peter now? He had abandoned his Friend and Lord and there could be no going back. Heartbroken and steeped in misery, he went back to the only life he had ever known before meeting Jesus, fishing. Some of the other disciples joined him. And then a beloved voice called from the beach.

> *Early in the morning, Jesus stood on the shore, but the*
> *disciples did not realize that it was Jesus. He called out to*
> *them, "Friends, haven't you any fish?" "No," they answered.*
> *He said, "Throw your net on the right side of the boat and*
> *you will find some." When they did, they were unable to*
> *haul the net in because of the large number of fish. Then*
> *the disciple whom Jesus loved said to Peter, "It is the Lord!"*
> *As soon as Simon Peter heard him say, "It is the Lord," he*
> *wrapped his outer garment around him (for he had taken*
> *it off) and jumped into the water (John 21:4-7 NIV).*

The God of the second chance had returned for His child. Peter was restored and went on to be one of the bedrocks of the church.

So, trim your sails and set out again. Just be sure He is in the boat with you.

46

In the Pit

I was sliding down into the pit of death, and he pulled me out.
He brought me up out of the mud and dirt. He set my feet on a rock.
He gave me a firm place to stand on.
(Psalm 40:2 NIV)

There is nothing worse than being in a pit of despair, wondering if you will ever get out, if the pain will ever go away, and if you will ever feel normal and happy again. Then to further complicate things, the "encouragers" arrive on the scene, making the situation go from bad to worse.

First along is the spiritual person who shouts down he will pray for you but then proceeds to hurry by. He considers his duty done and leaves with a clear conscience. He doesn't have time to stop because he is too busy serving God.

The next person is also very spiritual but, unlike the first person, she does stop for a minute to throw some scripture at you. She cries "the joy of the Lord is your strength," the inference being if you just stand on this bit of scripture you will be fine. Your response is "I know that, but how do I tap into joy when all I can feel is pain and anguish and my life is in pieces?"

The third person to come along tells you to have faith because without faith it is impossible to please Him. Now you feel even worse because apparently you are a weak Christian who cannot stand on the Word.

Now you worry if you can't dredge up the faith, does it mean God is going to leave you in the pit? And you sink further into despair.

Finally, a friendly voice shouts, "Hang on, I'm coming down. I've been there, and I know the way out. I will walk with you and guide you to the exit." This person actually descends into the pit and sits with you and listens, really listens, as you pour your heart out. Then he takes your hand, saying, "Let's go, I will lead. Just follow me."

When someone is struggling, she doesn't need words thrown at her. What she needs is someone who has been there, who has experienced her pain, and can truly appreciate her struggle. Often words are not even needed, just the presence of a warm, caring human being sitting with her is enough.

Joseph Bayly, who lost three sons, wrote about his grief in his book, *The View from a Hearse.*

> I was sitting, torn by grief. Someone came and talked to me of God's dealings, of why it happened, of hope beyond the grave. He talked constantly, he said things I knew were true. I was unmoved, except to wish he'd go away. He finally did.
>
> Another came and sat beside me. He didn't talk. He didn't ask leading questions. He just sat beside me for an hour or more, listened when I said something, answered briefly, prayed simply, left. I was moved. I was comforted. I hated to see him go. [1]

God shows us in the story of Elijah how He treats bruised, damaged people. The prophet was exhausted and despondent. He had run away into the wilderness and curled up under a bush in despair. He wanted

God to take his life (1 Kings 19:4). But God sent an angel to him who made him a meal and then told him to sleep some more. After he awoke the second time, the angel cooked him another meal. It was only after that did God start speaking to His prophet.

God knows we consist of both body and soul. That sometimes means we need rest and sustenance before the healing can begin, before we can stand on His Word and start the walk out of the pit.

> *A bruised reed He will not break, and a smoldering wick*
> *He will not snuff out (Isaiah 42:3 NIV).*

In Timothy Keller's book, *Walking with God Through Pain and Suffering*, he talks about this verse.

> The Hebrew word "bruise" does not mean a minor injury. It means a deep contusion that destroys a vital internal organ—a death blow. Applied to a person it means an injury that does not show on the surface but is nonetheless fatal. Suffering people need to be able to weep and pour out their hearts and not be shut down by being told what to do.[2]

Jesus always treated the bruised with gentleness and kindness. We should follow His example. Instead of throwing casual, worn-out phrases or scriptures at a hurting person, we need to get in the pit, take the time to sit with them, and listen. Only then, when they are ready, should we take their hand and lead them out.

If you are in the pit and none of your friends are coming for you, know there is one Friend who always will. When you are being led out of the pit, look down at the hand that is leading you. You may well find it is a nail-pierced one.

47

Dear "Younger Me"

And we know that all things work together for good to those who love God,
to those who are the called according to His purpose.
(Romans 8:28 NKJV)

The title of this piece is from a song by Mercy Me on their CD, "I Can Only Imagine."[1] The premise is if the songwriter could go back to in time to warn his younger self to avoid the mistakes he is going to make, would he do it?

I have listened to this song many times, but this time I stopped dead in my tracks as the depth of this thought suddenly sank in. If I was given the opportunity, would I go back and warn my younger self?

Then came one of the biggest "aha" moments of my life. I realized I would not. I would not go back and take the opportunity to warn my younger self because every mistake and every ounce of pain has made me what I am today and, most importantly, deepened my relationship with Christ. A God of love who held me every step of the way, even when I was not serving Him, who took every stupid mistake and situation and worked them for good.

I have a lot of scars, but I am proud of every one of them. They allow me to walk in another's shoes, they allow me to feel the pain someone else is going through because I have been there myself, and they give me the incredible privilege of being able to show His grace to the world.

So, "Younger Me," let me share this with you. You are going to go through some seriously tough stuff, and you are going to make some incredibly stupid mistakes. You are going to hurt to the point where you wonder if your heart can actually continue physically beating, and you are going to be deeply disillusioned.

But I am not going to do anything to prevent this because, through all these painful situations, you are going to meet the Person who willingly died for you, and you are going to experience a love beyond comprehension.

You are going to make it "Younger Me," so keep walking. The God who made the universe is going to take your very ordinary life and make it extraordinary because He is extraordinary.

48

Ordinary Days

There is still the youngest, Jesse replied.
But he's out in the fields watching the sheep and goats.
(1 Samuel 16:11 NLT)

O rdinary days. They can also be called the "blah" days. I'm talking about the days when nothing bad is happening, but nothing exciting is happening either. It's just business as usual. Same old, same old. On those days, we can be tempted to ask God, "Is this all there is, Lord?"

But it was on an ordinary day, when people were minding their own business and going about their daily work, that God suddenly moved. Unexpectedly, and with no warning, an ordinary day turned into an extraordinary one.

It was an ordinary day for David, who was tending his father's flocks, when Samuel, the prophet, arrived. He announced David was called to be anointed as the future king of Israel, much to the astonishment of all. And David was not just to be the future king of Israel. He was going to be the ancestor of the King of Kings, who would be known as the "Son of David."

Now Moses was tending the flock of Jethro his father-
in-law, the priest of Midian (Exodus 3:1 NKJV).

It was an ordinary day for Moses, who was taking care of his sheep in the wilderness, when the Lord called to him from the burning bush. Little did Moses know the years of taking care of a bunch of stubborn, recalcitrant sheep would be excellent training for what was coming—taking care of a bunch of stubborn, recalcitrant Hebrews and guiding them to the Promised Land.

> *Then Joshua son of Nun secretly sent two spies from Shittim. "Go, look over the land," he said, "especially Jericho." So they went and entered the house of a prostitute named Rahab and stayed there...So the king of Jericho sent this message to Rahab: "Bring out the men who came to you and entered your house, because they have come to spy out the whole land." But the woman had taken the two men and hidden them. She said, "Yes, the men came to me, but I did not know where they had come from. At dusk, when it was time to close the city gate, they left. I don't know which way they went (Joshua 2:1-5 NIV).*

It was an ordinary day for Rahab when the spies suddenly knocked on her door. She hid the spies, they reported back to Joshua, the walls of Jericho fell, and she became part of the genealogy of the Lord Jesus.

> *In the month of Nisan in the twentieth year of King Artaxerxes, when wine was brought for him, I took the wine and gave it to the king (Nehemiah 2:1 NKJV).*

It was an ordinary day for Nehemiah, who was working in the king's palace, when the Lord laid the plight of the sad state of the city of Jerusalem on his heart. Nehemiah had to ask the king to allow him to return to Jerusalem to rebuild the walls.

The angel of the Lord came and sat down under the oak in Ophrah that which belonged to Joash the Abiezrite, where his son Gideon was threshing wheat in a winepress to keep it from the Midianites. When the angel of the Lord appeared to Gideon, he said, "The Lord is with you, mighty warrior" (Judges 6:11-12) NIV.

It was an ordinary day for Gideon, who was threshing his crop in the winepress, hiding out from the Midianites, when the Angel of the Lord appeared to him to tell him he was going to be a judge and a deliverer of his people. Gideon was not thrilled at the prospect. When the Angel of the Lord referred to him as "mighty hero" he looked around to see who else the Angel could be talking to.

And Mordecai told them to answer Esther: "Do not think in your heart that you will escape in the king's palace any more than all the other Jews. For if you remain completely silent at this time, relief and deliverance will arise for the Jews from another place, but you and your father's house will perish. Yet who knows whether you have come to the kingdom for such a time as this?" (Esther 4:13-14 NKJV).

It was an ordinary day for Esther when Mordecai told her she needed to take her life in her hands and go to the king to save the Jews from the murderous plans of Haman.

Once when Zechariah's division was on duty and he was serving as priest before God, he was chosen by lot, according to the custom of the priesthood, to go into the temple of the Lord and burn incense...Then an angel of the Lord appeared to him, standing at the right side of the altar of incense (Luke 1:8-9; 11 NIV).

It was an ordinary day when Zechariah took his turn in the temple and an angel appeared to tell him John the Baptist would be his son and serve as the modern-day Elijah who would announce the coming of Jesus.

And Jesus, walking by the Sea of Galilee, saw two brothers, Simon called Peter, and Andrew his brother, casting a net into the sea; for they were fishermen (Matthew 4:18 NKJV).

It was an ordinary day for Peter, Andrew, James, and John, mending their nets after a night's fishing, when the Lord called them to follow Him. That ordinary day started them on the path to the glory of our Lord's resurrection.

Meanwhile, Saul was still breathing out murderous threats against the Lord's disciples. He went to the high priest and asked him for letters to the synagogues in Damascus, so that if he found any there who belonged to the Way, whether men or women, he might take them as prisoners to Jerusalem. As he neared Damascus on his journey, suddenly a light from heaven flashed around him. He fell to the ground and heard a voice say to him, "Saul, Saul, why do you persecute me?" (Acts 9:1-4 NIV).

It was an ordinary day for Saul when the Lord stopped him dead in his tracks on the road to Damascus. He was reborn as the apostle Paul.

Ordinary people doing ordinary things on ordinary days. The common thread is do not scorn ordinary days. They are often a precursor to God moving.

49

God Has a Sense of Humor

Then I said, "Put a clean turban on his head."
So, they put a clean turban on his head and clothed him,
while the angel of the Lord stood by.
(Zechariah 3:5 NIV)

God has a sense of humor. I know this for a fact. He made me. And ducks and donkeys and pelicans. Duck-billed platypuses too. I defy you to watch a duck waddling to a pond and not smile.

But I also have personal proof of His humor. I had surgery which resulted in my head being bandaged in a big, white turban. The kindest comment I got from my loving family was that I looked like a character from the children's show, the Teletubbies! Friends and co-workers amused themselves by sending me character hats—one in the shape of the shark head from the *Jaws* poster, with teeth framing my face, a bonnet with fruit and flowers, a squid. They also offered a lot of annoying suggestions.

After a night of pain and very little sleep, I woke up extremely irritated and not in the mood for talking to anyone. When I looked in the mirror, my mood worsened. The turban was now loose with bandages dangling everywhere. I looked like a swollen mummy coming unwrapped. A large area of the bandages was also covered in blood stains. It was a delightful picture. I decided to avoid checking messages and emails, choosing instead to spend time with Someone who I knew would understand my pain and misery.

That was when I discovered God really does have a sense of humor. I opened my Bible and looked down at this verse in Zechariah, where the Lord is telling Joshua the High Priest to go put on a clean turban. I didn't land on a passage about healing or the Lord being my strength through long, painful nights. Instead, I landed on a passage talking about a turban. You can decide whether this was just a coincidence or the Holy Spirit having some fun. I think He was encouraging me to laugh with him.

And, of course, He did once use a donkey to deliver His prophetic message.

50

The Fifth Sparrow

Are not five sparrows sold for two pennies?
Yet not one of them is forgotten by God.
(Luke 12:6 NIV)

The going rate to purchase sparrows in Jesus' day was one penny for two sparrows and two pennies for five sparrows. The fifth sparrow was thrown in free.[1]

Do you sometimes feel like a fifth sparrow? Unimportant, just thrown into the world as an afterthought, perhaps not really needed and worth little?

This verse shows us God remembers even one little sparrow. He made that sparrow, He loves that sparrow, and He takes care of that one little sparrow the world might think is worth nothing. The fifth sparrow is just as important and valuable as the other four in God's eyes.

> *Yet not one of them will fall to the ground outside of your*
> *Father's care (Matthew 10:29 NIV).*

You are not a forgotten fifth sparrow. You are a one-of-a-kind, fearfully and wonderfully made, unique in every way sparrow.

For You formed my inward parts; you covered me in my mother's womb. I will praise You, for I am fearfully and wonderfully made... My frame was not hidden from You, when I was made in secret, and skillfully wrought in the lowest parts of the earth. Your eyes saw my substance, being yet unformed. And in Your book, they all were written, the days fashioned for me, when as yet there were none of them (Psalm 139:13-16 NKJV).

You are a masterpiece. The dictionary definition of a masterpiece is "a person's greatest piece of work, a consummate example of skill or excellence of any kind."[2]

For we are God's masterpiece. He has created us anew in Christ Jesus, so we can do good things he planned for us long ago (Ephesians 2:10 NLT).

Don't ever think you are a mistake or an accident.

Before I formed you in the womb, I knew you (Jeremiah 1:5 NKJV).

You are created in God's own image.

So, God created man in His own image; in the image of God He created him; male and female He created them (Genesis 1:27 NKJV)

And God has marvelous plans for your life.

For I know the thoughts that I think toward you, says the Lord, thoughts of peace and not of evil, to give you a future and a hope (Jeremiah 29:11 NKJV).

So, stand proud little sparrow. Your Father in heaven adores you and is watching carefully over you as you wing your way through life.

51

Crooked Halos

But God has chosen the foolish things of the world to put to shame the wise,
and God has chosen the weak things of the world to put to shame the things which are mighty.
(1 Corinthians 1:27 NKJV)

I f you ever stop and wonder if God can use you with all the mistakes and missteps in your life, simply go look at the people He used in the Bible. It will give you great comfort. There is not a straight halo amongst them. In fact, good luck finding a halo at all.

- Abraham started out life worshipping idols. God built a nation on him.
- Jacob was a liar and a deceiver. His descendants became the twelve tribes of Israel.
- Moses murdered an Egyptian. God used him to lead His people to the Promised Land.
- Rahab was a harlot, but if you read the genealogy in Matthew 1, she shows up as Christ's great, great (not sure how many greats) grandmother. (Those genealogies make interesting reading when you see who God thought was good enough to be used to bring His Son into the world).
- David committed adultery and arranged the death of an innocent man. God refers to him as a man after His own heart.

- Jephthah was the son of a harlot, not an auspicious start in life. God used him as one of the judges of Israel.
- Jonah hopped onto a ship going in the opposite direction to where God wanted him to be (apparently, he thought God might not notice) and landed in a whale. Yet God still used him to prophesy to Nineveh and the nation was saved.
- Elijah ran away, plopped down next to a stream, threw a pity party, and asked God to kill him. God had other plans. Instead, Elijah never saw death and went to heaven in a chariot of fire.
- John Mark gave up in the mission field and caused a major split between Paul and Barnabas. Barnabas wanted to give him a second chance; Paul was having none of it. Barnabas was proved right. John Mark went on to serve Christ and a gospel bears his name.
- Matthew was a tax collector who ripped off his own people. He became an apostle.
- Paul murdered God's people. Then he ran head-first into Christ on the road to Damascus. He wrote two-thirds of the New Testament.
- Peter denied the Lord three times and was restored. Although I suspect every time he heard a rooster crow he probably twitched. Jesus even came to him and served him breakfast on the beach.

There are so many people who can be added to the list, but you get the drift. God uses damaged, battle-scarred people to further his works. Because in the end it is about Him, not you.

52

Not Manna Again!

Then the Lord said to Moses, "Behold, I will rain bread from
heaven for you.
And the people shall go out and gather a certain quota every day,
that I may test them, whether they will walk in My law or not."
(Exodus 16:4 NKJV)

I have had jobs that were incredibly tedious. I have had jobs that
were exciting and adrenalin fueled, but even those had periods of
boredom and monotony. It was during one of these boring times, when
I was grousing and complaining about the situation, I read the story of
the Exodus.

The book of Exodus recounts the trials and travels of the Israelites as they
wandered in the desert before entering the Promised Land. They were
confused and frightened, but God provided for them in every possible
way. He led them by a pillar of cloud during the day and by a pillar of
fire every night. Their shoes did not wear out, they stayed healthy, and
He provided water and sustenance whenever they needed it. Yet the
Israelites still complained and whined despite having all the necessities
of life. Sound familiar?

The commentary I was reading alongside the verse above pointed out the
piece most of us probably miss—"*that I may test them.*" Manna wasn't
sent simply as a supply to keep them alive; it was a test from God.

Every day for forty years, God faithfully sent the manna. Manna every day—boiled, baked, barbecued, broiled, basted, buttered, battered— always manna. God provided it, not only for their bodies, but as a test of their patience, perseverance, and day-in and day-out obedience. They did not pass the test. Their complaints resulted in them getting bombarded with quails – kind of – taking a bit of poetic license here.

God never ever lets an experience go to waste. He uses those slow, tedious times to build our patience and perseverance. As this sank into my brain, I realized I needed to ask God for forgiveness for whining and, more importantly, to thank Him for what He has given me. Before I get hit on the head by a bird.

53

Betrayal

Even my own familiar friend in whom I trusted, who ate my bread, has
lifted up his heel against me.
(Psalm 41:9 NKJV)

I t is believed David penned this about his trusted counsellor, Ahithopel, who turned against him and betrayed him when David's son, Absalom, rose up against his father in an attempt to usurp the throne.

At some point in life, it is likely we will suffer the sting of betrayal from a friend, a co-worker, even a spouse, and it will cut deep. However, betrayal can have a positive effect. The hurt, heartache, and disillusionment can bring you closer to God if you don't allow bitterness and anger to set in.

I went through a situation where I was horribly betrayed by someone I thought was a friend, and I struggled to understand why God had let it happen. Why hadn't He protected me?

Then, while reading the book *Detours* by Tony Evans, I came across something that turned my thinking completely on its head. He said God often uses negative experiences to accelerate our spiritual growth and push us further along the path to the destiny He has in store for us.[1]

When Joseph landed in prison, he could easily have blamed Potiphar's wife for putting him there. But Mrs. Potiphar was simply the instrument used to place him in the prison, which was exactly where God needed Joseph to be in order to further prepare him for his ultimate destiny—being second in command in Egypt. Through Joseph came the saving of a nation along with Joseph's family, the family which would become the seed the nation of Israel would grow from and the line that would bring Jesus into the world.

Jesus suffered the ultimate betrayal by a friend, and worse, it was accompanied by a kiss. A kiss, which in those times denoted love and respect, became an action of mockery and death.

> *I do not speak concerning all of you. I know whom I have chosen; but that the Scripture may be fulfilled, "He who eats bread with Me has lifted up his heel against Me" (John 13:18 NKJV).*

It's interesting to note that when Jesus quoted this line from the psalm, He left out the phrase, "in whom I trusted." He knew from the beginning that Judas would betray Him. Thankfully, we will never have to suffer betrayal at that level.

Don't get angry or bitter toward those who have hurt you. They do not know it but God is using their bad behavior for your ultimate good. Jesus is our faithful Friend. He will never betray us, never leave us, never forsake us. His loyalty and love can never be questioned. He will always remain by our side.

> *And we know that in all things God works for the good of those who love him, who have been called according to his purpose (Romans 8:28 NKJV).*

Neither should you engage in payback, no matter how hurt or angry you are. Vengeance belongs to God and to Him only. If anything needs to be done, He will handle it in His perfect timing and in exactly the right measure. Do not let hurt poison your heart and hold you back from allowing God to fulfil His plan for your life. Jesus told us we have to forgive just as He forgave us. We can NEVER give more grace than He has already given us.

> *For by grace you have been saved through faith, and that not of yourselves; it is the gift of God (Ephesians 2:8 NKJV).*

Betrayal can sometimes feel like death; death of hope and trust. After Jesus' betrayal, He died on the cross but on the third day came resurrection. He will resurrect your hopes and your dreams and heal your wounds. Cling to His hand. Resurrection Sunday is on the way!

54

The Valley of Baca

Blessed is the man whose strength is in You,
Whose heart is set on pilgrimage.
As they pass through the Valley of Baca,
They make it a spring;
The rain also covers it with pools.
They go from strength to strength;
Each one appears before God in Zion.
(Psalm 84:5-7 NKJV)

The Valley of Baca (the valley of tears) is a place that symbolizes hopelessness and despair. We all go through our personal valleys of Baca, those difficult, painful places in life where everything seems hopeless and we feel helpless.

The Baca tree is a balsam tree that produces resin. It is harvested by making small cuts in the branches. The tree then bleeds a sap which hardens into tear-shaped drops.

It's important to note a word in this scripture, *"through."* They pass through the valley; they do not make camp and live there. God always brings us through our trials.

Even though I walk through the darkest valley, I will fear no evil, for you are with me; your rod and your staff, they comfort me (Psalm 23:4 NIV).

Through the water, *through* the rivers, *through* the fire. Throughout the Bible, God is always delivering His people through.

When you pass through the waters I will be with you; and when you pass through the rivers they will not sweep over you. When you walk through the fire, you will not be burned; the flames will not set you ablaze (Isaiah 43:2 NIV).

God not only brings us through the valley, He is in the valley with us. And He will bring us safely out the other side. Hold on and keep walking. You will not remain there, and you will receive a blessing from the experience.

Weeping may endure for a night but joy comes in the morning (Psalm 30:5 NKJV).

55

Wounded Souls

The souls of the wounded cry out.
(Job 24:12 NKJV)

I s your soul wounded? Your heart pierced? Are you bruised? Are you battered? Are you bleeding? Have you given up on hope?

Some wounds cut deep, and you wonder if it is possible for them to ever completely heal. You silently keep walking but you continue to bleed, slowly and sluggishly.

This particular injury is deep because the blow landed from someone you trusted and respected. Someone to whom you were vulnerable. Someone you may even have loved.

Worse, the blow came from someone in the body of Christ. You were injured by someone in your own family. The ones who are supposed to protect and look out for you. Still worse, he walked away without even a backward look. He was totally uncaring about the damage and heartache he left in his wake.

Now you look at your family in Christ and wonder which one is going to be next—the next one to use you, hurt you, and then drop you like a used tissue.

But there is one Person who knows what it is like to be betrayed by a friend. He experienced the ultimate betrayal, and for a pathetic thirty pieces of silver. No matter our hurts, we will never suffer betrayal at that level.

So go to Him, hold onto His Hand. He understands the pain and confusion. He will bring you through. He will bring you peace and healing. He did it for me. He will do it for you.

> *He heals the brokenhearted and binds up their wounds*
> *(Psalm 147:3 NKJV).*

56

The Black Dog

Even though I walk through the darkest valley,
I will fear no evil, for you are with me.
(Psalm 23:4 NIV)

Hemingway referred to it as "the black dog." As did Winston Churchill. Both suffered from severe depression. I know what they are talking about. I have battled depression on and off for over thirty years.

Sometimes it comes as a dark, black cloud that quietly sinks down over you. Other times it is more insidious. Instead of a black cloud, it is a soft, gray mist that envelops you. The sun may physically be shining, but life is monochrome and blah, like the English countryside on a rainy day.

For those of us who have had to deal with this malady, we are in exceptional company. Some of the greatest saints in the Bible dealt with this issue. A good example is Elijah. He was so depressed he begged at one point for the Lord to take his life.

> *And he prayed that he might die, and said, It is enough!*
> *Now, Lord, take my life, for I am no better than my*
> *fathers! (1 Kings 19:4 NKJV).*

Luckily, God did not grant Elijah's prayer and continued to use him mightily. So much so that Elijah never saw death. God took him directly to heaven in a chariot of fire.

Even the man who wrote two-thirds of the New Testament was not immune. Despite his road to Damascus experience, despite being taken three times into the third heaven into the very presence of God, despite being trained personally by the Holy Spirit in Arabia for three years, Paul fell into a well of despair. He had faced intense spiritual battles; been physically beaten, whipped, and scourged; had often gone hungry and thirsty; and carried a weight of worry on his shoulders for his beloved church. Finally, weary and drained, he hit bottom.

> *We were under great pressure, far beyond our ability to endure, so that we despaired of life itself*
> *(2 Corinthians 1:8 NIV).*

Often, to add to your misery while you are dealing with the black cloud or the gray mist, the voice will come telling you that you are never going to make it, that it is just too hard, that things are never going to change, that it is always going be like this.

Do not listen to that hissing sound. That isn't your Shepherd speaking. That is the Enemy's vile voice. Your Shepherd is right there next to you. Reach out, take His hand, and He will walk you safely through the valley out into the sunshine on the other side. God has a plan for your life and all the forces of darkness cannot stop what He has ordained.

> *I know that You can do anything and no plan of Yours can be thwarted (Job 42:2 HSCB).*

For the Lord of All has planned, and who can keep it from happening? Who can turn His hand back? (Isaiah 14:27 NLV).

57

The Eleventh Hour

Then He said to Jesus, "Lord, remember me when
You come into your kingdom."
(Luke 23:42 NKJV)

R ecently, a friend's sister passed away. In her lifetime, her sister had not, to her knowledge, accepted Christ. She had prayed for her sister's salvation, but now the end had come, and she was left with the terrible fear that her sister had not made it to heaven. She was also carrying enormous guilt that perhaps she should have done more, prayed harder, or been more persuasive in her arguments.

While she was speaking, the thief on the cross came to mind. Nailed to a cross, dying, he looked over at the beaten, bloody body of the One who had committed no crime and who was now dying on his behalf. In that moment, the man glimpsed salvation. He asked Jesus to remember him when Jesus came into His kingdom. Not the most eloquent prayer, not one based on years of theology, but a cry from deep down in his soul, with I think, little hope.

And through His pain and torment, Jesus raised his head and looked into the eyes of His child and said, *"Assuredly, I say to you, today you will be with Me in paradise"* (Luke 23:43 NKJV).

At the eleventh hour, Jesus reached out and pulled a dirty, damaged, crippled sheep safely into the sheep pen just as the door was closing. The penitent thief entered heaven with a smile and a dance in his step. He was forgiven and saved, which can be summed up in one word—grace.

We have no idea what happens in those last minutes of life. We do know God does not want to lose even one of His flock. In the parable of the lost sheep, Jesus said, *"What man of you, having a hundred sheep, if he has lost one of them, does not leave the ninety-nine in the wilderness, and go after the one which is lost until he finds it?" (Luke 15:4 NIV).*

He repeats this message in the parable of the lost coin. *"And when she finds it, she calls her friends and neighbors together and says, 'Rejoice with me; I have found my lost coin.' In the same way, I tell you, there is rejoicing in the presence of the angels of God over one sinner who repents" (Luke 15:9-10 NIV).*

I have no doubt He is with the dying giving them the chance of a last-minute reprieve. I am sure my friend's prayers were heard, and He pulled her sister into the sheepfold just as the door was closing.

58

Attrition of the Soul

He drew me up from the desolate pit, out of the miry bog,
and set my feet upon a rock, making my steps secure.
(Psalm 40:2 NRSV)

I read an excerpt from *The Screwtape Letters* by C.S. Lewis, where Screwtape was giving his revolting nephew, Wormwood, advice on how to overcome the Christian by "using time to wear down the soul." He tells Wormwood that long, dull, monotonous years are "excellent campaigning weather."

And, unfortunately, he's right. We are at our most vulnerable during those seasons when we feel like we have been walking and walking and nothing seems to be breaking.

Boy, do I know that feeling. I had been walking through what felt like a never-ending season of struggle and waiting. I knew He had something up the road for me, and I knew I needed to keep standing and walking, but the drab, monotonous days filled with dull pain seemed to be never ending and the light at the end of the tunnel was very dim.

It was like walking in a quagmire, where each step felt like I was sinking into a morass of mud. It was a major effort to free myself from the sucking sludge. I could almost hear the squelching, plopping sound as it reluctantly released my foot, only to suck me back down again on the next step. And when I looked up, there appeared to be nothing but miles of mud ahead of me.

It is during these times, when we are tired from fighting the ooze, when we have been walking and walking and walking, that the Enemy arrives on the scene. He knows a weakened, weary, worn-out adversary is easy to bring down.

This is exactly the time we need to dig deep, grab onto Jesus' hand with everything we've got, and keep going. He will reach down and pull us up from the pit. I love the Voice version of Psalm 40:2. It shows God's heart towards us and His loving care during these times.

> *He reached down and drew me from the deep, dark hole where I was stranded, mired in the muck and clay. With a gentle hand, He pulled me out to set me down safely on a warm rock; He held me until I was steady enough to continue the journey again.*

He holds us in the palm of His hand, *"For I, the Lord your God, will hold your right hand, saying 'Fear not, I will help you'"* (Isaiah 41:13 NKJV). He engraves our name on his palms, *"Behold, I have indelibly imprinted (tattooed a picture of you) on the palm of each of My hands"* (Isaiah 49:16 AMPC).

God is our ever-faithful Shepherd leading us safely through the valley of death and shadows to the sunlight and green pastures on the other side.

> *Even when I walk through the darkest valley, I fear no danger because you are with me. Your rod and your staff— they protect me (Psalm 23:4 CEB).*

Don't believe the lies of the Enemy who whispers God has forgotten you as you walk through the long monotonous days. Our Lord is right there beside you and, more importantly, He is constantly working on your behalf. You may not see anything happening, but trust me, it is. He is bringing His plan for your life to fruition in a way that will amaze and astound you.

Don't let a miserable creature like Wormwood win!

59

Whatever You Do, Don't Run

When visiting Africa, it is a good idea to take note of the following tips when dealing with the local wildlife.

1. Stay in your vehicle. This seems like a no-brainer, but it's amazing how many people blithely hop out of their vehicles to take a closer look at the big kitty only to experience disastrous results.

2. If you are unfortunate enough to meet up with an African predator while on foot, stand your ground. Human beings are not the natural prey for most predators. When the animal sees you, a question mark will form in its brain. What exactly is this creature? Is it safe to go after? Is it edible and digestible? Will it fight back? As long as you stay still, that question will remain unanswered and the animal may (I said may) walk away. However, the minute you turn and run, you have just proven beyond a shadow of doubt that you are, in fact, prey because only prey runs. The question mark is now replaced with an exclamation mark; "yay, dinner time!"

3. If you happen to come across a cute, baby animal wandering around, do not try to pet it or rescue it. Freeze. Study the surroundings carefully. That baby animal is most likely going to have a mom or pop close by who will be quite happy to bite you or stomp on you for going too close to their little darling.

4. Don't ever mess with vultures. Not quite sure why you would, but people do weird things. Their first line of defense is to vomit. And we all know what vultures eat!

5. If chased by a leopard, don't climb a tree. They climb faster and more efficiently than you ever could. I have no idea how you handle this particular scenario; I suggest prayer. A short one will suffice, "Help, Lord."

6. Hippos are the most dangerous animals in Africa. Yes, I know that does not make sense when there are large crocodiles lying around on sandbanks, but they are. More people die at the hands (hooves?) of hippos than any other creature. They are ornery, usually in a bad mood, and extremely territorial. They are also extremely fast and agile in water; they can chase down a boat and sink it in minutes. They are pretty fast on land too. So treat them with great respect, and, if you do inadvertently wander into their territory, depart quickly and quietly.

7. If charged by a rhinoceros, stand your ground and jump out of the way at the last minute. Due to their bulky bodies, rhinos can't make last minute corrections to swerve to the side. I've never tried this myself, nor do I know anyone who has, but if that happens to you, I suggest you try this method. And if you survive, let me know so I can update this page.

I am sure you are wondering what tips on surviving in Africa has to do with your Christian walk. Actually pretty much nothing. I just threw this in for fun.

Although, there are two spiritual principles you can apply to your Christian walk. See item 2 "Stand" and item 5 "Pray."

60

Let Down Your Net One More Time

When he had finished speaking, he said to Simon,
"Put out into deep water and let down the nets for a catch."
(Luke 5:4 NIV)

P eter was tired. The night spent fishing had resulted in nothing but a wet net. So, when the young rabbi approached and asked if He could use Peter's boat, Peter was willing to do just that. Pushing a boat a little way out into the sea so the rabbi could more easily teach the crowds wasn't a big deal.

But when the rabbi told Peter to put to sea and let down his nets again, Peter's willingness evaporated. First, everyone knew, except apparently this rabbi, that you don't catch fish during the day. Second, Peter and his crew had already been fishing for hours and had caught nothing but bits of seaweed. And, third, Peter had already cleaned the nets to prepare them for the next night. Yet something made Peter obey, and we all know the end to the story. Peter got the biggest catch (and fright) of his life and ended up face down in a bunch of smelly fish declaring Jesus Christ as Lord.

Sometimes we reach a point where we just feel too spent to let down our nets again. Despite all efforts, the marriage problems continue with no sign of a breakthrough; the wayward kid is once more standing on your last nerve; the job search is fruitless since no one seems to want to hire an older person or a young, inexperienced one; or the illness that has sapped your spirit and exhausted your body has returned. You are left feeling hopeless and too tired to keep going.

As hard as it may be to do, obey the young Rabbi. Let your net down one more time. This could be the day you get the catch that will change your life.

61

The Heart of the Father

Anyone who has seen Me, has seen the Father.
(John 14:9 NIV)

Christ is the visible image of the invisible God.
(Colossians 1:15 NLT)

My Dad died when I was ten. Prior to that, he was a remote figure who kissed me goodbye in the morning before he left for the office and good night when I went to bed in the evening. I have no memory of him spending any quality time with me; no spontaneous hugs, no conversation. After I became a Christian, I realized I was having a serious struggle with getting to know the Father.

Jesus wasn't a problem. He was the loving older brother who I could go to with everything. He was kind and understanding; someone who was always there for me, who would put His arms around me and take care of me, who would dry my tears.

God was the stern, remote father in his study at the end of a long, dark hallway, much like the hall to the principal's office at my school.

Many years later, a pastor told me the reason I had such a hard time understanding the love of my heavenly Father was because I had no real idea of the love of an earthly father. Growing up with a dad who was remote and, then, who disappeared completely out of my life, had left a gaping hole. In his book, *The Case for Grace*, Lee Strobel uses the term "an orphan in the heart" in one of his stories.[1] That hit home with me. That's what I was, an orphan in the heart. So, between having a remote dad and a mom who was not the "touchy-feely" type, I grew up with few demonstrations of love or words of affection.

I read the scriptures about God being a God of love. My mind accepted the premise, but it never sank into my heart. My perceptions always stayed the same; God the Son was the approachable one, God the Father was not. Then, many years later, I came across Max Lucado's books and, thanks to him, I finally grasped the love of an earthly father and was able to translate it into the love of my heavenly Father.

Max Lucado often talks about his daughters and recounts stories of them growing up. One of the stories that resonated with me was when his daughter, Jenna, was giving a piano recital and had a mental block. Her fingers froze on the keyboard in front of the audience and she couldn't continue. After agonizing minutes, she finally got back on track and bravely finished the piece but the damage was done. Lip quivering and tears welling, she came off stage and into the arms of her dad, who hugged her and told her everything was okay.[2] After reading that, the scripture *"He who has seen Me, has seen the Father"* finally moved from head to heart then spirit.

At that moment, my entire walk with God changed. Everything started falling into place. Now I could pray openly without being afraid. I could tell God the Father anything. Thanks to Max Lucado, my entire Christian walk moved to a deeper level.

62

Kingdom Perspective

For every animal of the forest is mine, and the cattle on a thousand hills.
(Psalm 50:10 NIV)

Nothing I have is mine. All is given to me by Him. Therefore, it is my duty to share all that I have. Simple. That is kingdom perspective.

We now have "Giving Tuesday," a movement to create an international day of charitable giving. It falls after "Black Friday" and "Cyber Monday" which are all about consumerism. "Giving Tuesday" is a breath of fresh air in an increasingly commercialized Christmas season. It makes us stop and think of those who are less fortunate, and gives us the opportunity to help.

But the Christmas season is also a time when the demands on our heartstrings and purse strings grow often causing anxiety to set in. How much do we give? Who should we be giving to? How can we give to everyone, although we wish we could? Will we have enough for our own needs if we do give?

The answer is to rely on the Holy Spirit to lead us to give in the right amount at the right time. We can rest in Him and give without fear, knowing He will take care of all our needs.

But my God shall supply all your need according to his riches in glory by Christ Jesus (Philippians 4:19 NKJV).

Your heavenly Father already knows all your needs. Seek the Kingdom of God above all else, and live righteously, and he will give you everything you need (Matthew 6:32-33 NLT).

63

Our Lighthouse

In Him was life, and that life was the light of all mankind.
The light shines in the darkness, and the darkness has not overcome it.
(John 1:4-5 NIV)

I grew up in Cape Town, South Africa where life revolves around the ocean. Lots of fun times were spent swimming in the sea and playing on the beach. Dolphins and whales made regular appearances as did Great White sharks on occasion. (That's somewhat less fun. It's amazing how fast you can swim when a fin is sighted. I became quite adept at identifying fins, a curved fin = dolphin; a triangular fin = shark). However, the oceans around the tip of Africa have a more ominous side. Violent storms blow up suddenly, and many a ship has gone to its doom on the rocks around the coast. Its moniker "Cape of Storms" was not given lightly.

As a child, I watched the rescue of a cargo ship, the *Sea Farer,* which went onto the rocks during a storm less than two hundred feet off the promenade. Miraculously, there was no loss of life. I still remember the helicopters battling back and forth in gale force winds lifting people to safety and the massive waves buffeting the broken ship.

The stanchion that saved many ships from a similar fate was a small, red-and-white striped lighthouse. It blared its horn and sent its beam of light out into the darkness to warn ships they were approaching danger and needed to change course. Its light also guided lost sea farers to shore.

Jesus is our red-and-white striped lighthouse. When the storm suddenly comes upon us, with gale force winds raging, rain pounding, and waves threatening as we desperately try to find land, His light will beam out through the darkness, and He will guide us safely to shore.

His light not only saves us, it also warns us of impending danger. Just as the light from the lighthouse warns ships of the hidden shoals, His Word will keep us safe when we are in danger of veering off the path.

> *Your word is a lamp to my feet and a light to my path (Psalm 119:105 NKJV).*

64

The Walls Will Fall

And the seventh time it happened, when the priests blew the trumpets,
that Joshua said to the people:
"Shout, for the Lord has given you the city!"
And it happened when the people heard the sound of the trumpet,
and the people shouted with a great shout, that the wall fell down flat.
(Joshua 6:16; 20 NKJV)

Jericho. Joshua's stronghold was immense and well-fortified. The city was built on a tall mount of land, surrounded by an earthen embankment. It had two walls with a space in between; the outer one was six feet thick, the inner one was twelve feet thick. The walls were so broad chariots could race on top.

Our Jerichos are just as intimidating. They come in the form of sickness, despair, fear, negativity, anxiety, anger, bitterness, barrenness, addictions, and more. Jericho must fall for you to move into your promised land.

God said to Joshua, "receive the city I have taken for you," not "go take the city." God has already won the ground for you. The Commander of angel armies has gone ahead of you and won the victory on your behalf. Your part is to take it.

For though we walk in the flesh, we do not war according
to the flesh. For the weapons of our warfare are not

carnal but mighty in God for pulling down strongholds (2 Corinthians 10:3-4 NKJV).

The definition of a stronghold is a conviction, outlook, or belief that attempts to interfere with the truth. A stronghold in terms of our Christian life is a false premise that denies God's promise. [1]

Every battle is first won in the spiritual realm before it manifests in the physical. Your weapons of war are praise, worship, the Word, and prayer.

The word "trumpet" means ram's horn in the original Hebrew. The ram's horn was blown to celebrate a victory already won. The silver trumpet was used to call the people to assemble *(Numbers 10:2)*.

Joshua knew the walls would come down on the seventh day, but nowhere does it say he told the Israelites that. They were told to just march and keep on marching. Sometimes God does the same with us. He guarantees the wall will come down, but He doesn't say when. And so, you walk, and walk, and walk ....

Sometimes you will experience a metaphorical six days of weary trudging around the walls, but the seventh day will come, and the walls will fall. Your Jericho will come down. Blow your ram's horn!

65

The God of "I Will!"

I will guide you along the best pathway for your life.
I will advise you and watch over you.
(Psalm 32:8 NLT)

One morning during my quiet time, I met the God of "I will." I'd been struggling through a valley of depression and was tired and despondent. So I told Him how I felt, honestly and truthfully, no holds barred. God knows what's in my heart anyway, so there is no point in trying to hide it. He is big enough to handle my doubts and questions. He knows I love and trust Him. The fact I can come to Him and tell Him I am not okay is proof of that.

He answered as I flipped through my Bible. Scripture after scripture of "I WILL" came before me. Not "I may" or "I could" but "I WILL." The emphasis in each verse below is mine.

> *The Lord WILL fight for you; you need only to be still (Exodus 14:14 NIV).*

> *He gives strength to the weary and increases the power of the weak. But those who hope in the Lord, WILL renew their strength. They WILL soar on wings like eagles; they WILL run and not grow weary, they WILL walk and not be faint (Isaiah 40:29, 31 NIV).*

And I WILL give you a new heart – I WILL give you new and right desires - and put a new spirit within you (Ezekiel 36:26 TLB).

I am with you and WILL watch over you wherever you go (Genesis 28:15 NIV).

I WILL instruct you and teach you in the way you should go; I WILL guide you with My eye (Psalm 32:8 NKJV).

You WILL keep in perfect peace all who trust in You, all whose thoughts are fixed on you (Isaiah 26:3 NLT).

No matter how dark the outlook is or how despondent you are, He WILL come to you. He WILL take care of you. He WILL comfort you. He WILL guide you. He WILL!

66

He Cares for the Animals

A righteous man regards the life of his animal.
(Proverbs 12:10 NKJV)

God loves animals. He created them, He populated the Garden of Eden with them, and He instructed Adam to take care of them. Throughout the Bible, God's concern for animals is shown.

After the flood, He made a covenant, not only with Noah, but with the animals as well.

> *Then God said to Noah and to his sons with him: "I now establish my covenant with you and with your descendants after you and with every living creature that was with you—the birds, the livestock and all the wild animals, all those that came out of the ark with you—every living creature on earth. I establish my covenant with you: Never again will all life be destroyed by the waters of a flood; never again will there be a flood to destroy the earth"* (Genesis 9:8-12 NIV).

In Deuteronomy 25:4, He instructs the Israelites not to muzzle the ox while it is threshing: *"You shall not muzzle an ox while it treads out the grain."* In other kinds of labor, oxen were muzzled. But here God instructs the farmer not to do that. It is only right the animal be allowed to eat some of the fruit of its labors. God shows not only His care for the animal here, but also uses it as a teaching symbol for people to be kind to their servants and laborers. He instructed the people to, not only rest themselves, but to let their animals rest as well:

> *"Six days you shall do your work, and the seventh day you shall rest, that your ox and your donkey may rest"* *(Exodus 23:12 NKJV).*

In Jonah, He regarded the life of the animals.

> *"And should I not pity Nineveh, that great city, in which are more than one hundred and twenty thousand persons who cannot discern between their right hand and their left—and much livestock?" (Jonah 4:11 NKJV).*

A Christian should take care of God's creatures if he calls himself a Christian. Righteousness includes taking care of animals, be it your own animal, some poor creature being abused or ill-treated, or a wild one. These are God's creatures, and we will be held accountable for how we take care of them on His behalf. I seriously question someone who calls themselves a Christian but ill-treats His creatures.

> *For every animal of the forest is mine, and the cattle on a thousand hills. I know every bird in the mountains, and the insects in the fields are mine (Psalm 50:10-11 NIV).*

He regards every creature as valuable. He even hears when a single raven calls out for food.

> *He gives food to the wild animals and feeds the young ravens when they cry (Psalm 147:9 NLT).*

Aren't two sparrows sold for only a penny? But your Father knows when any one of them falls to the ground (Matthew 10:29 CEV).

In Habakkuk, God called down judgement on those who destroyed trees and animals and killed humans.

"You cut down the forests of Lebanon—now you will be cut down! You terrified the wild animals you caught in your traps—now terror will strike you because of all your murdering and violence in cities everywhere" (Habakkuk 2:17 TLB).

A friend recently found a turtle lying in the road, injured and bleeding. I am going to give the person who hit it and then drove on the benefit of the doubt. Maybe he was not aware he had run into the poor thing. My friend demonstrated the true heart of God. She scooped it up, wept tears over its pain, and took it to an animal clinic for medical care.

(I cannot give you a scripture that irrefutably proves that animals go to heaven, but there are many Christian authors who believe they do, including C.S. Lewis, Randy Alcorn, James Herriot, and dozens of others, as well as many Christian pastors and theologians. Needless to say, I believe animals go to heaven. Feel free to argue with me. I will point out you were wrong when we are in heaven and my animals are sitting at my feet.)

67

God, the Ultimate Artist

Then God said, "Let the waters abound with an
abundance of living creatures,
and let birds fly above the earth across the face of the
firmament of the heavens."
(Genesis 1:20 NKJV)

When I look at nature and the incredible creatures inhabiting our world, I stand awed and amazed by the work of His hands. He did not have to put so much effort into making each creature unique and spectacular, but He did. He designed and painted the world for His pleasure and for ours. He is the Ultimate Artist.

- He gave the platypus a Donald Duck smile and the duck a waddle in its walk.
- He gave the cheetah its spots and speed and the lion its magnificent mane and roar.
- He gave the hyena its laugh and the nightingale its melody.
- He gave the cockatoo its crest and the peacock its breathtaking tail.
- He gave the whales their song and the eagles their flight.
- He gave the zebra its stripes and painted the goldfinch yellow.
- He gave the pelican its pouch and the marlin its spike.

Creation is God's first missionary. How can you possibly look at the multitude and variations of animals on earth, or at the heavens and the stars, and not accept there is a God? He reveals Himself to mankind through His creation. His handiwork is clear for all to see. And His creation is breath taking and spectacular, expressing the magnificence of the Creator Himself.

> *For ever since the world was created, people have seen the earth and sky. Through everything God made, they can clearly see his invisible qualities--his eternal power and divine nature. So, they have no excuse for not knowing God (Romans 1:20 NLT).*

68

The Two Lions

Be careful—watch out for attacks from Satan, your great enemy.
He prowls around like a hungry, roaring lion, looking for
some victim to tear apart.
(1 Peter 5:8 TLB)

I am from Africa and have been up close and personal with lions. A male lion can weigh over 500 pounds. They are not cute, cuddly pussy cats. They are powerful, dangerous animals, and we are no match for them. Even a "tame" one can revert to type very quickly. You need to treat these creatures with great respect. Stupidity and casualness will get you killed.

When visiting lion parks in South Africa, there are signs everywhere instructing you to drive slowly. If you don't, it aggravates the lions lying by the side of the road and they may swipe at your tires with their paws. Their claws are so lethal they can shred a tire in seconds. You often see tourists with deflated tires and deflated egos waiting for rescue by the game keepers. And usually there is a lion lying nearby with a smug look on its face.

In our Christian walk, there are two lions. One is the cowardly lion, who lurks in the shadows and pounces when he sees an opportunity. The good news, however, is that there is a second lion. This Lion overcame Satan and because of Him we do not have to walk in fear. The Lion of Judah has won the victory for us and He bears scars on His paws as proof of that.

Our modern culture has made Satan into a cartoon character. He's portrayed capering around on hooves with pointed horns, holding a trident, and surrounded by the flames of hell. He is nothing like that.

Satan is a powerful enemy; he is pure evil, and he has been around for eons. He has had millennia to hone his craft. He plays dirty and he plays for keeps. He has studied you carefully and he knows your weaknesses. And he often presents himself as an angel of light.

Originally, he was called Lucifer (Isaiah 14) and was the most beautiful angel created—a radiant, shining, glorious being. In Ezekiel it says, "*you were the seal of perfection, full of wisdom and perfect in beauty. The workmanship of your timbrels and pipes was prepared for you on the day you were created*" (*Ezekiel 28:12-13 NKJV*). It appears that Lucifer orchestrated worship in heaven, but he became so enamored with his own beauty he tried to make himself equal with God.

> *For you have said in your heart: "I will ascend into heaven, I will exalt my throne above the stars of God; I will also sit on the mount of the congregation on the farthest sides of the north; I will ascend above the heights of the clouds, I will be like the Most High (Isaiah 14:13-14 NKJV).*

> *Your heart was lifted up because of your beauty; you corrupted your wisdom for the sake of your splendor (Ezekiel 28:17 NKJV).*

After he tried to make himself like God, Lucifer was cast out of the third heaven and fell to earth where he now holds court. One-third of God's angels followed him into rebellion and fell with him. Lucifer is not confined to hell; he is free to roam the earth as legally it is his—for the moment. He also has access to God. He appears in front of the throne where he accuses the brethren.

> *One day the angels came to present themselves before the Lord, and Satan also came with them (Job 1:6 NIV).*

> *On another day, the sons of God came to present themselves before the Lord; and Satan also came with them to present himself before Him (Job 2:1 NIV).*

The good news is that Christ has won the victory against Satan on our behalf. He defanged and declawed our adversary at the Cross.

> *And I heard a loud voice in heaven, saying, "Now the salvation and the power and the kingdom of our God and the authority of his Christ have come, for the accuser of our brothers has been thrown down, who accuses them day and night before our God" (Revelation 12:10 ESV).*

However, you had better know your place in Christ if you want to successfully win the battle with Satan and his minions. Invoking the name of Jesus like a magic talisman is not going to work. You must know Him and who you are in Him. The seven sons of Sceva learned this truth the hard way. They tried to use the name of Jesus to exorcise some evil spirits, but they did not know Him and the result was pandemonium.

> *And the evil spirit answered and said, "Jesus I know, and Paul I know; but who are you?" Then the man in whom the evil spirit was leaped on them, overpowered them, and prevailed against them, so they fled out of that house naked and wounded (Acts 19:15-17 NKJV).*

So, be alert but don't be afraid. Satan is only loose for a season and that season is short.

> *He is filled with fury, because he knows that his time is short (Revelation 12:12 NIV).*

We overcome him by:

- The Cross. *"Having wiped out the handwriting of requirements that was against us, which was contrary to us. And he has taken it out of the way, having nailed it to the cross. Having disarmed principalities and powers, He made a public spectacle of them, triumphing over them in it" (Colossians 2:14-15 NKJV).*
- The Blood. *"And they overcame him by the blood of the Lamb and by the word of their testimony, and they did not love their lives to the death" (Revelation 12:11 NKJV).*
- The Name. *"Therefore, God also has highly exalted Him and given Him the name which is above every name, that at the name of Jesus every knee should bow, of those in heaven, and of those on earth, and of those under the earth" (Philippians 2:9-10 NKJV).*
- The Word. *"Put on the whole armor of God, that you may be able to stand against the wiles of the devil. And take the helmet of salvation, and the sword of the Spirit, which is the word of God" (Ephesians 6:11, 17 NKJV).*

Keep your eyes on the Lion of Judah and the cowardly lion lurking in the shadows will not be able to come near.

> *Therefore submit to God. Resist the devil and he will flee from you (James 4:7 NKJV).*

69

Roots

Blessed is the man who trusts in the Lord
And whose hope is the Lord.
For he shall be like a tree planted by the waters,
Which spreads out its roots by the river,
and will not fear when heat comes;
But its leaf will be green
And will not be anxious in the year of drought,
Nor will cease from yielding fruit.
(Jeremiah 17:7-8 NKJV)

Hardly anyone pays attention to the roots of a tree. They're hidden underground, out of sight and out of mind. When they do break the surface, they are not considered particularly attractive.

The top of the tree, the part visible to the world, is what catches the eye—thick green foliage, sometimes beautiful blossoms—but the roots we ignore and undervalue. Without those strong roots, however, the tree cannot grow, cannot blossom, and cannot provide shade or a home for the birds. If it puts down puny roots, the first storm that comes its way will take it down. And this is a perfect analogy for our Christian lives.

Jesus warned that the house built on sand would be washed away, that the seed scattered on hard ground would not take, and that the Christian without strong roots would fall.

Some fell on stony ground, where it did not have much earth; and immediately it sprang up because it had no depth of earth. But when the sun was up it was scorched, and because it had no root it withered away (Mark 4:5-6 NKJV).

But the ones on the rock are those who, when they hear, receive the word with joy; and these have no root, who believe for a while and in time of temptation fall away (Luke 8:13 NKJV).

These likewise are the ones sown on stony ground who, when they hear the word, immediately receive it with gladness; and they have no root in themselves, and so endure only for a time. Afterward, when tribulation or persecution arises for the word's sake, immediately they stumble (Mark 4:16-17 NKJV).

But when the sun was up, they were scorched, and because they had no root they withered away (Matthew 13:6 NKJV).

When trials come, and they will, if we are not firmly rooted in His Word, we will fall over like the shallow-rooted tree. Having strong roots doesn't mean we won't struggle and stumble or question and cry. It means that underneath it all will be the firm, unshakeable assurance that God has us in His Hand, that He will never leave us nor forsake us, and that He will bring us through because His Word is underpinning us.

As you therefore have received Christ Jesus the Lord, so walk in Him, rooted and built up in Him and established in the faith, as you have been taught, abounding in it with thanksgiving (Colossians 2:6-7 NKJV).

70

What's in a Name?

I will reveal My Name to My people, and they will
come to know its power.
(Isaiah 52:6 NLT)

God places enormous emphasis on names. He regards them as so important He often changed a person's name when He called them.

Abraham, meaning "father of a multitude," was originally Abram or "exalted father." Sarah, meaning "princess," was originally Sarai. Jacob's name meant "grabber of the heel" or "deceitful." His new name, Israel, meant "one who prevails." Joshua, which means "Jehovah saves" or "the Lord is salvation," was originally named Hosea. Saul, after his experience with the risen Lord on the road to Damascus, became Paul. And Jesus renamed Simon, Cephas, which means Peter.

Thinking about this, it dawned on me that I do not go by any of my birth names. I did not revert to my maiden name after my divorce, and I shorten my first name from Patricia to Pat. Patricia comes from the Latin and means "noble one." Pat is a description of a spread, as in a "pat of butter," or the word for a demonstrative gesture, as in a "pat on the back." Less appealing is "cow pat." I think I need to start going by Patricia. My exceptionally talented webmaster goes by the name of Lisa, which means "the Lord is bountiful."

A name represents the character of the person behind it, and through His names (over eighty-five are listed in the Bible) God reveals His nature to us. Each name is related to His ability to meet our needs, and by giving us His different names, He shows us He is our All in All. No matter what our situation or need, He is able to meet it.

> *In the beginning God (Elohim) created the heavens and the earth (Genesis 1:1 NKJV).*

We meet Elohim, our all-powerful, creator God in the first verse of Genesis. God opened His Word, revealing Himself in majesty and power. Mountainous peaks sprang into being at His word and the waters rolled back to their allotted boundaries at His command. Elohim is also plural reminding us it was the Triune God who created all things, the Father, the Son, and the Holy Spirit. When you need an all-powerful God, one who can move mountains with a word, call on Elohim.

> *This is the account of the heavens and the earth when they were created, in the day that the Lord God made earth and heaven (Genesis 2:4 NASB).*

In Genesis 2, we meet Jehovah God (Yahweh), our personal, relational, interactive, and covenantal God. Yahweh (YHWH) was the name the Jews regarded too sacred to be spoken. When God wants to emphasize His relationship with man, He always uses the name Jehovah, and whenever you see the word LORD in capitals in your Bible, it is a translation of Yahweh.

> *The Lord is my Shepherd; I shall not want. He makes me to lie down in green pastures; He leads me beside the still waters. He restores my soul; He leads me in the paths of righteousness for His Name's sake (Psalm 23:1-3 NKJV).*

When you are walking through a dark valley, call on Jehovah Rohi, the Lord your Shepherd. He will take your hand and lead you safely out.

> *I will put none of the diseases on you which I have brought on the Egyptians. For I am the Lord who heals you (Exodus 15:26 NKJV).*

If you need physical or emotional healing, call on Jehovah Rapha, the Lord your Healer.

> *And Abraham called the name of the place, The-Lord-Will-Provide (Genesis 22:14 NKJV).*

Abraham met the Lord Who Provides at the altar when the Lord gave him a ram as a sacrificial replacement for Isaac. When you need provision, call on Jehovah Jireh, the Lord your Provider.

> *So, Gideon built an altar there to the Lord, and called it The-Lord-Is-Peace (Judges 6:24 NKJV).*

When the storms rage and the waves crash over your head, that is when you call on Jehovah Shalom, the Lord Your Peace, and He will calm your heart. He may even come to you, like He did for Peter, walking on the water.

> *And Moses built an altar and called its name, The-Lord-Is-My-Banner (Exodus 17:15 NKJV).*

In the time of Moses, banners weren't like the banners we see today. They were the insignias at the top of the poles carried by the Israelites to identify the tribes. Joshua met the "Lord Our Banner" when the pre-incarnate Jesus appeared to him as the Commander of Angel Armies (Joshua

5:14). When we go into battle, He goes ahead of us. Call on Jehovah Nissi when you are marching into the battle.

> *Now this is His name by which He will be called: The-Lord-Our-Righteousness (Jeremiah 23:6 NKJV).*

This name occurs only twice in the Old Testament (Jeremiah 23:6 and Jeremiah 33:16). When you have slipped and fallen, and are in need of forgiveness, run to Jehovah Tsidkenu, the Lord your Righteousness.

> *For he made him who knew no sin to be sin for us, that we might become the righteousness of God in Him (2 Corinthians 5:21 NKJV).*

Jesus is our righteousness. We don't stand clothed in our own, but in His, purchased at the cross through the shedding of His blood.

> *Then she called the name of the Lord who spoke to her, You-Are-The-God-Who-Sees; for she said, "Have I also here seen Him who sees me?" (Genesis 16:13 NKJV).*

When Hagar fled into the wilderness to escape Sarah's cruelty, alone and frightened, seemingly abandoned, the Angel of the Lord came to her, the God Who Sees saw her. He sees you in your pain and abandonment and will come to you when you call on Jehovah Roi, the God Who Sees.

The final name I include is Immanuel, meaning God With Us. This is His incarnational name, the name that embodies and fulfils all the other names. It is "The Name above all Names," Jesus.

Whatever your need, God has a name that speaks directly to that need. Whatever your situation, call on His name and He will answer. He is there for you in every way—perfectly.

71

Wait

*I am weary with my crying; my throat is parched;
my eyes fail while I wait for my God.
(Psalm 69:3 NASB)*

Wait is the scariest word in the Bible for me. It also happens to be a four-letter word, which I deem totally appropriate. Never mind pestilence, disease, judgement, crawling locusts, and famine. Wait is the one that makes my heart sink. Sometimes God makes you wait and wait and wait.

If you are sitting in His waiting room, waiting for His call, take comfort from this. Many people in the Bible who were used mightily by God had long periods of waiting.

Abraham waited seventeen years for Isaac (with a slight detour by the name of Ishmael along the way).

Moses waited forty years in the desert tending a bunch of smelly sheep before his calling.

Joseph waited seventeen years to ascend to his position as Pharaoh's second-in-command, two of which were spent in prison.

Daniel waited for twenty-one agonizing days before the angel Gabriel broke through.

Paul was sent to Arabia for three years to learn from the Lord before being let loose on the world.

David also waited. After being anointed by Samuel, he went right back to the sheep pasture. So much for being the future king of Israel. He had to go back to a bunch of dumb animals, and not just any animals, sheep—critters constantly in need of protection and care. But this turned out to be excellent training for a future king who would have to take care of his subjects. And years passed before he finally became king, many of which were spent in a cave.

> *Rest in the Lord, wait patiently for Him; do not fret*
> *(Psalm 37:7 NIV).*

There is a difference between sitting around doing nothing and waiting on God. Waiting is active, not passive. Wait with excited anticipation for what He is bringing about. Just because you cannot see what is going on, it does not mean He is doing nothing. The Israelites stood on the shore of the Red Sea seeing nothing but waves ahead of them and an army of Egyptians coming from behind. What they couldn't see was God working behind the scenes. He is working behind the scenes for you too. Always remember, your future does not only include you; it includes others and is part of a greater plan God is putting into place. Whatever He is doing will bring glory to Him.

When the days get long and strength gets weak, go to Isaiah 40:31 and hold on to His promise.

But those who wait on the Lord, shall renew their strength;
They shall mount up with wings like eagles, they shall run
and not be weary, they shall walk and not faint (NKJV).

And when it finally all comes about, you will be amazed at the perfection of both His plan and His timing.

72

The Advantage of Height

For my thoughts are not your thoughts, and My ways are not your ways,
says the Lord.
For as the heavens are higher than the earth, so are My ways higher
than your ways
and My thoughts than your thoughts"
(Isaiah 55:8-9 NKJV)

I had spent most of the day hurling a ball across the garden for four small dogs to retrieve. The plan was to get them tired so the humans could have a peaceful afternoon while the dogs recovered from their exertions. The dogs would bounce happily after the ball, but sometimes they couldn't find it in the high grass. They would search around, tails frantically wagging, trying to recover it. Eventually, they would give up and expectantly look to me for help. They knew I would find it for them because I had an advantage over them—height.

Being taller, I had a wider perspective and that got me thinking. So often we do what the dogs do—go frantically searching for the answer to the problem when what we really need is Someone taller and situated higher than us, who can see the whole aspect of the situation and give us the solution from His vantage point.

> *It is He who sits above the circle of the earth, and its inhab-*
> *itants are like grasshoppers, who stretches out the heavens*

182

*like a curtain, and spreads them out like a tent to dwell
in (Isaiah 40:22 NKJV).*

Our perspective is earth bound. We can see only one frame at a time in
the movie of our life. But God can see it all, from beginning to end. He
wrote the script before we were born. He knows exactly what needs to
be done to move us forward.

*Before I formed you in the womb, I knew you, before you
were born, I set you apart (Jeremiah 1:5 NIV).*

When you are confused about a situation and don't know what to do,
take a step back and let Him show you it from His viewpoint. He will
also show you the step you need to take to move out of the long grass
and onto the path He has for you.

73

An Army of Sheep

You are my sheep, the sheep of my pasture, and I am your God,
declares the Sovereign Lord.
(Ezekiel 34:31 NIV)

Alexander the Great said, "I am not afraid of an army of lions led by a sheep; I am afraid of an army of sheep led by a lion."

Alexander would have been terrified of the army of God because we are an army of sheep led by the most powerful lion in the universe, the Lion of Judah. When we become Christians, whether we like it or not, we are drafted into His army. No true Christian gets to sit on the sidelines and watch the action.

> *Fight the good fight of faith (1 Timothy 6:12 NIV).*

> *You therefore must endure hardship as a good soldier of Jesus Christ (2 Timothy 2:3 NKJV).*

> *No one engaged in warfare entangles himself with the affairs of this life, that he may please Him who enlisted Him as a soldier (2 Timothy 2:4 NKJV).*

Some Christians make the decision to straggle along at the back of the pack, more camp followers than soldiers. Satan pays attention to all

Christians, but it is the Christian marching into battle that makes him really sit up and take notice. He will occasionally lob a hand grenade into the path of the camp followers and assign a few lazy demons to cause trouble, but it is the other group that he keeps his laser-like focus on. The Christian who causes the greatest disruption in his dark kingdom is the one who takes the great commission seriously and reaches out to a dying world, preaching the cross of Christ and singing praises to the King of Kings.

Satan is a powerful enemy, but we don't have to be intimidated or afraid because Christ has already won the war on our behalf. We may get weary on the march, we may get wounded in a skirmish, but we can never be overcome because we are held safely in the palm of our Lord's hand. Our victory is assured.

The Bible tells us that our war is not with flesh and blood but with principalities and powers.

> *Finally, my brethren, be strong in the Lord and in the*
> *power of His might. Put on the whole armor of God, that*
> *you may be able to stand against the wiles of the devil.*
> *For we do not wrestle against flesh and blood, but against*
> *principalities, against powers, against the rulers of the*
> *darkness of this age, against spiritual hosts of wickedness*
> *in the heavenly places (Ephesians 6:10-12 NKJV).*

At the cross, Jesus disarmed those principalities and powers, and took back the keys of death from Satan.

> *Having disarmed principalities and powers, He made*
> *a public spectacle of them, triumphing over them in it*
> *(Colossians 2:15 NKJV).*

To march in God's army, however, we need to put on the armor and take up the weapons He has provided for us, otherwise we will be a bunch of sitting ducks, easy to pick off. Paul based his description of God's given armor on the armor of the soldiers of the Roman Empire. People saw these soldiers daily and would have clearly understood the analogy.

> *Therefore, take up the whole armor of God, that you may be able to withstand in the evil day, and having done all, to stand. Stand therefore, having girded your waist with truth, having put on the breastplate of righteousness, and having shod your feet with the preparation of the gospel of peace; above all, taking the shield of faith with which you will be able to quench all the fiery darts of the wicked one. And take the helmet of salvation, and the sword of the Spirit, which is the word of God (Ephesians 6:13-17 NKJV).*

Girdle of Truth - the girdle Roman soldiers wore was a thick, heavy, leather band that held the soldier's sword and other weapons. Without Biblical truth as the basis of our lives, we are unprotected and completely open to the Enemy's attacks. We also need the girdle to hold our Sword of the Spirit.

Breastplate of Righteousness – the Roman soldier's breastplate protected his heart and other internal organs. The breastplate symbolizes our righteousness in Christ. It is His righteousness, purchased for us at the cross, that protects us. Faith and love also protect our hearts.

> *But let us who are of the day be sober, putting on the breastplate of faith and love, and as a helmet the hope of salvation (1 Thessalonians 5:8 NKJV).*

Shoes of the Gospel of Peace – the Roman soldier wore sandals with hobnails in the soles to keep him surefooted in battle and less prone to slip. To stand surefooted in the war, we need His shoes of peace. When the storms blow, His peace will keep us steady and upright.

> *You will keep him in perfect peace, whose mind is stayed on You, because he trusts in You (Isaiah 26:3 NKJV).*

Shield of Faith – this part of our armor is something we must take up. Unlike the previous three pieces of armor which we wear, this one requires effort. The Roman shield (scutum) was a large, rectangular shield about three and a half feet tall by three feet wide. The soldier could pretty much cover his whole body with it.

The description of faith is given in Hebrews, *"Now faith is the substance of things hoped for, the evidence of things not seen" (Hebrews 11:1 NKJV).* To take up the shield of faith is to actively trust God and His Word. In Roman times, the enemy would sometimes shoot arrows, dipped in flammable substances and lit on fire. Satan will try to send his "fiery darts" our way, but we can dowse them by faith.

Helmet of Salvation – Satan loves to attack the mind. You must let your mind be controlled by God's Word. Satan cannot lead a believer astray who mind is stayed on God.

Sword of the Spirit - all the armor of God is defensive in nature, except the Sword of the Spirit. This is our only offensive weapon and is the only offensive weapon we need because it is the Word of God. Jesus gave us an example of the use of this weapon when He defeated Satan in the wilderness by wielding the Sword of the Spirit, the Word.

> *For the word of God is living and powerful, and sharper than any two-edged sword, piercing even to the division*

of soul and spirit, and of joints and marrow, and is a discerner of the thoughts and intents of the heart (Hebrews 4:12 NKJV).

Keep your weapons and your armor at the ready all the time. And at the end of the age, when Christ returns, we will be part of his victorious heavenly army.

Now I saw heaven opened, and behold, a white horse. And He who sat on him was called Faithful and True, and in righteousness He judges and makes war. His eyes were like a flame of fire, and on His head were many crowns. He had a name written that no one knew except Himself. He was clothed with a robe dipped in blood, and His name is called The Word of God. And the armies in heaven, clothed in fine linen, white and clean, followed Him on white horses. Now out of His mouth goes a sharp sword, that with it He should strike the nations. And He Himself will rule them with a rod of iron. He Himself treads the winepress of the fierceness and wrath of Almighty God. And He has on His robe and on His thigh a name written: KING OF KINGS AND LORD OF LORDS (Revelation 19:11-16 NKJV).

74

Plant and Water

I planted, Apollos watered, but God gave the increase.
So then neither he who plants is anything, nor he who waters,
but God who gives the increase.
(1 Corinthians 3:6-7 NKJV)

Sometimes we plant and sometimes we water. Sounds a little like the country song lyrics "sometimes you're the bug, sometimes you're the windshield."[1] Sometimes you may sow a seed which someone else will be tasked with watering, or you may be the one watering a seed planted by someone else.

We often get stressed about evangelizing, but we can rest secure in the knowledge it is the Holy Spirit who does the work. Our part is to simply be His instrument, learn to hear His gentle whisper, then do what He tells us to do. He goes before us and prepares people's hearts; He does the saving and He does all the work. Our eloquent speech or brilliant delivery achieves nothing without Him. Paul was not great with words, as he admits in Corinthians, but he turned the world on fire for the gospel.

> *For some say, "His letters are weighty and forceful, but in person he is unimpressive and his speaking amounts to nothing" (2 Corinthians 10:10 NIV).*

189

It is the voice of the Holy Spirit combined with the Word of God that releases the power of God to save.

God can and will use whatever resource is available to reach someone or get their attention. He has used a large fish (Jonah), a donkey (Balaam), and a burning bush (Moses). He will use the beauty of a sunset or, as in the case of C.S. Lewis, a person who does not believe in Him at all.

C.S. Lewis was struggling with the concept of Christianity. He had reached the point of accepting that there is a God, but the Christian belief of a God that died for him was a bridge too far. Then the words of a professor friend, T.D. Weldon, who was looking at the life of Christ, stopped him in his tracks. Weldon threw out a random comment, "Rum thing, that stuff of Fraser's about the Dying God, it almost looks as if it really happened once." Those words so shocked Lewis he could not get them out of his mind. Between that, and the various conversations he had with his Christian friends, including J.R. Tolkien, finally brought him to Christ. God used an atheist to reach him.

St. Augustine did not start out life as a saint. His life was "colorful" to put it nicely. One day, he heard the voice of a child singing, "Pick it up and read it. Pick it up and read it." It occurred to him that this could be a command from God, so he found a Bible and opened it. The first passage he saw was, *"Let us behave properly as in the day, not in carousing and drunkenness, not in sexual promiscuity and sensuality, not in strife and jealousy. But put on the Lord Jesus Christ and make no provision for the flesh in regard to its lusts" (Romans 13:13-14 NASB).* Augustine said reading that scripture made his heart flood with life. He totally turned from sin to pursue the things of God and ended up with the word "saint" before his name.

D.L. Moody did not attend school beyond the fifth grade. His education was sadly lacking; he couldn't spell and his grammar was appalling. He never became an ordained minister. But through the patient kindness of his Sunday school teacher, Edward Kimball, he finally came to Christ. It is believed that Moody may have led a million or more souls to the Lord.

A snowstorm helped lead C.H. Spurgeon to Christ. At the age of fifteen, a snowstorm stopped him in his tracks, causing him to seek shelter in a Methodist chapel. Only a dozen or so people showed up for service and the minister never made it. But one deacon who had made it to church that morning felt that as people had braved the storm to get there, they should hear a sermon. So he preached. Not well, however. It was dry and convoluted. He preached this text from Isaiah, *"Look unto me, and be ye saved, all the ends of the earth: for I am God, and there is none else" (Isaiah 45:22 KJV)*. He looked down at Spurgeon from the pulpit and shouted to him, "Young man, look to Jesus Christ." That was the moment in Spurgeon's words that, "there and then the cloud was gone, the darkness had rolled away, and that moment I saw the sun." Spurgeon became known as the "Prince of Preachers."

A seed is packed with amazing power. It will push aside a mountain to reach the sun. So plant and water. The results could be astounding. You could be the instrument that unleashes another Spurgeon or a Billy Graham on the world.

75

Words Need Action

Suppose a brother or a sister is without clothes and daily food. If one of you says to them, "Go in peace; keep warm and well fed," but does nothing about their physical needs, what good is it?
(James 2:15-16 NIV).

You will notice something when you read the Gospels. Almost every time Jesus performed a miracle, it was combined with an action.

Then Jesus put out His hand and touched him, saying, "I am willing; be cleansed" (Matthew 8:3 NKJV).

When He cleansed the leper, He could have done it with just a word, but He touched the man. That touch did not just heal the man physically, it healed him emotionally. A leper was considered an outcast of the outcasts. His diagnosis doomed him to a life of loneliness and isolation. He had to avoid people and cry out "unclean, unclean" wherever he walked. He was cast out from his family, no longer permitted to feel the touch of a loved one or receive hugs from his children. He was shunned and looked upon with horror and scorn. Picture then, after such years of anguish and misery, a hand of love and kindness reaching out and touching that leper. Can you imagine what that must have felt like?

And He said to her, "Daughter, your faith has made you
well. Go in peace and be healed of your affliction" (Mark
5: 34 NKJV).

When Jesus healed the woman with the issue of blood *(Mark 5:21-34).*
He could have simply walked on after He felt her touch the hem of
His garment. But He turned and called her out. Her medical problem
would have affected every part of her life. It made her unclean, which
meant she could not touch her husband or children. She would not have
been allowed in the temple and would have been socially ostracized. She
would not even have been allowed to take care of her own home because
anything she touched would also have been deemed unclean. Jesus not
only restored her health, but through His touch He restored her socially.

When He raised Jairus' daughter from the dead, He followed it up with
a practical action. He told them to get her something to eat. *"Then He*
took the child by the hand and said ... arise. Immediately the girl arose and
walked ... He commanded them strictly that no one should know it and
said that something should be given her to eat" (Mark 5:41-43 NKJV).

When He healed the two blind men, He touched them. *"Then He*
touched their eyes, saying, 'according to your faith let it be to you'" (Matthew
9:29 NKJV).

When He healed Peter's mother-in-law, He touched her. *"So, He came*
and took her by the hand and lifted her up, and immediately the fever left
her" (Mark 1:31 NKJV).

The list goes on and on, but the message is clear. Words need action. That
not only applies to our interaction with people, it also applies to how
we share the gospel and tell the world about Christ. Whoever we touch,
Jesus touches. When we comfort someone, we need to touch them and
walk with them through their pain.

In her book, *Out of the Saltshaker and Into the World,* Rebecca Manley Pippert reminds us we don't "give" the gospel, we "are" the gospel; we don't "do" evangelism, we "are" evangelism; and whomever we touch, Jesus touches. [1] We are the only Bible some people will ever read, and we are the only Jesus some people may ever meet. Our actions and our behavior present Jesus to the world. That is an awesome responsibility that literally could mean life or death.

Words and action—a practice we Christians need to emulate.

76

I Was Lost, But Now I'm Found

*Then Jesus told them this parable: "Suppose one of you has a hundred
sheep and loses one of them.
Doesn't he leave the ninety-nine in the open country and go after the lost
sheep until he finds it?
And when he finds it, he joyfully puts it on his shoulders and goes home."
(Luke 15:3-7 NIV)*

My precious cat, Sammy, went missing one day. He was a big softie, in no way equipped to deal with the dangerous world beyond the confines of his comfortable home. I was in a total panic, frantically searching the neighborhood. I walked for hours calling his name, looking under every bush and up every tree, into every culvert and drain, asking every neighbor I met if they had seen him. For two long days I desperately searched for him, with little sleep, going out at daybreak each day.

Then it occurred to me. Isn't this how Jesus searches for us, His lost sheep? He walks day and night, searching the valleys and mountainside, calling our names, His voice becoming hoarse, His eyes scratchy and sore from dust and pollen, His legs scarred by the scratches of brambles and bushes, but never giving up.

And once Jesus find us, He never lets us go. He saves us, seals us with His Holy Spirit, writes our names on the palms of His hands and in the

195

Lamb's book of life. In doing so, He sends a very clear message to the Enemy, "This child is Mine, hands off!"

I finally found Sammy. He was upstairs in my neighbor's condo. She had gone away for the weekend and had left the door open while carrying her luggage to the car. Sammy's curiosity got the better of him and he slipped in unnoticed. He had spent two days ten feet above my head. My neighbor also had a cat, so Sammy had food, water, a kitty box, and plenty of soft surfaces to recline on. He had a vacation while I had a breakdown!

77

The Survivor Tree

Therefore, if anyone is in Christ, he is a new creation;
old things have passed away;
behold, all things have become new.
(2 Corinthians 5:17 NKJV)

September 11, 2001 is a day marked in infamy on par with the attack on Pearl Harbor. It's a day that no one who lived through could ever forget. The twin towers falling, the Pentagon burning, and the lone plane crashing in a remote field in Pennsylvania taken down by incredible people who decided they would rather give their own lives than see others die. In John 15:13, Jesus said, *"Greater love has no one than this, than to lay down one's life for his friends."* Those people exemplified that love.

Every day I drive past the Pentagon to and from work—a building that usually represents strength and permanence. Until September 11th, that is. Coming home that afternoon, I could see the huge gaping hole in the side and the charred skeleton of the plane that had become a missile. I could smell the ghastly odor of burning jet fuel. The sounds of sirens seemed to continue for hours as injured survivors were pulled from the burning rubble and rushed to nearby hospitals.

I was working for two former New York congressmen at the time. That morning, we all watched in horror as the twin towers fell. Both knew people who worked in those buildings. It was confirmed later some of the people they knew did not make it out.

But despite the incredible evil that was perpetrated that day, stories and images of unbelievable courage and bravery stood above it all.

There was the story of a man who dug in the rubble for days without sleep or rest until he found the body of his firefighter son who had gone into the buildings to rescue people. There was the image of police officers and firemen standing to attention, saluting as the body of a German Shepherd dog was brought out on a stretcher. He had gone into the tower with his policeman handler and had died by his partner's side. Story after story of ordinary people working the pile, day in and day out, determined to bring loved ones home to their families.

There is one simple but special story that made me pause and think. On the site was a small pear tree. When the buildings fell, it was buried under tons of rubble. As the rescuers went about the ghastly task of recovering bodies, they came across the little tree, severely damaged, crushed, and burned. On a regular day, it probably would have been tossed aside, headed for the garbage dump. But the workers didn't see a crushed tree, they saw hope. They carefully dug it up and handed it over to the New York City Department of Parks and Recreation for rehabilitation.

Miraculously, the tree survived, grew, and flourished. But the most amazing thing about the tree is that there is a clear demarcation between its past and its present. One side of the tree is gnarled, scarred, and burnt. The other side is new, green, budding, and growing. It became known as the "Survivor Tree" and it is now part of the 911 memorial at Ground Zero.

Isn't that how we were before we came to Christ? Broken, gnarled, burnt, with no hope for the future, ready to be tossed aside on life's garbage heap. But then Christ comes and makes all things new, and we grow and flourish, our burnt pasts left behind.

78

Yertle the Turtle

(With apologies for Dr. Seuss for appropriating his title)

I have set before you life and death, blessings and curses.
Choose life so that you and your descendants may live.
(Deuteronomy 30:19 NRSV)

I live adjacent to a creek that attracts a lot of wildlife, including turtles. One morning, I came upon a large turtle crossing the four-lane street next to the creek. It was making its way towards a construction area on the opposite side of the road, heading straight into piles of brick and rubble with not even a puddle of water in sight.

It could not have made its way up the steep, overhanging, rocky embankment so my guess was someone had found it in the river and brought it up onto the grass verge. I will make no comment on the common sense of this person.

The turtle seemed oblivious to the fact that behind it was a stream with clear, babbling water and lush vegetation. It just kept plodding on with great determination and, for a turtle, at quite a speed.

After rescuing it from the road, sliding down the embankment to the water's edge and placing it back in the stream, I watched it swim off happily and, to my delight, be joined by another turtle further down-stream.

Sitting in my car afterwards, stained with turtle pee (yes, it thanked me by peeing on me on the way down the embankment), it occurred to me I had just witnessed a great picture of us before salvation.

We determinedly follow our own path, heading into a desert of dust and rubble, with certain death at the end, ignoring the living water Christ so freely offers us and the green valley of rest He provides.

> *He makes me to lie down in green pastures; He leads me*
> *beside the still waters (Psalm 23:2-3 NKJV).*

Let Him lead you beside still waters and restore your soul. Follow the path that leads to life.

79

If You Ever Doubt His Love

For God so loved the world that He gave His only begotten Son,
that whoever believes in Him should not perish but have everlasting life.
(John 3:16 NKJV)

Most of us have asked this question at some time or another, when darkness and pain is overwhelming and there doesn't appear to be an end in sight. "Where are You, Lord? Do you really care?"

To answer this, I will simply point you to the cross. You cannot spend time at the foot of the cross, meditating on what He did, and leave doubting His love for you.

He could have come at a kinder period in history – when executions were carried out with bullets or guillotines, when death was comparatively quick and merciful. Instead, He came when the method of execution was violent and cruel. But His timing was perfect and purposeful.

Here is a description of death on a cross during Roman times. Who would voluntarily offer themselves up to this?

Before the cross came the scourging. Jesus was whipped with a "flagrum," a whip with long leather tails that had bits of sheep bone or small bits of metal braided into them, which would cut deep into His skin and subcutaneous tissues. As the flogging continued, the lacerations would have become so deep they would have reached the underlying skeletal muscles, resulting in long ribbons of bleeding flesh. A scourging typically resulted in rib fractures and bruising of the lungs, with bleeding into the chest cavity. The Romans were experts at this form of torture and knew exactly how to inflict the most damage without killing the person. Jesus would have been bleeding and trembling with shock when he was returned to Pilate. No wonder He couldn't carry His cross to Golgotha and Simon the Cyrene had to be conscripted to carry it for him.

Then came the crucifixion. Death on a cross was usually a result of excessive blood loss, traumatic shock, or cardiac and respiratory arrest.

Victims were nailed to the cross through the hand at the base of the palm and at an angle so that the nail came out through the wrist. This would support the body's weight but also cause excruciating pain. Hanging by the arms results in the pectoral muscles becoming paralyzed, making the intercostal muscles unable to act. Air can be drawn into the lungs but not exhaled. Jesus would have had to push up on His legs to try to breathe. (The reason legs were often broken was to hasten death because the person would no longer be able to push up and, thus, would die more quickly from suffocation.) This horrific cycle of pushing up and then sinking down would have continued for hours as He struggled to breathe. The movement up and down against the rough wood of the cross would have exacerbated the pain from the deep lacerations in His back. His pericardium would slowly have filled with blood and compressed his heart.[1]

That's just the physical description of the pain of the crucifixion and what led up to it. Add to this the indescribable agony of being separated from His father, the Trinity being torn apart, and the unspeakable horror of taking the sins of all mankind on Himself so that we might live.

In spite of His agony, He asked the Father to forgive those who were crucifying Him. He heard the repentant plea of the thief hanging beside Him and pulled Him safely into the Kingdom just as the gates were closing. He also remembered His mother and consigned her safely into the care of His beloved disciple, John.

> *Then Jesus said, "Father, forgive them, for they do not know what they do" (Luke 23:34 NKJV).*

> *Then he said to Jesus, "Lord, remember me when You come into Your kingdom." And Jesus said to him, "Assuredly, I say to you, today you will be with Me in Paradise" (Luke 23:42-43 NKJV).*

> *When Jesus saw his mother there, and the disciple whom he loved standing nearby, he said to her, "Woman, here is your son," and to the disciple, "Here is your mother." From that time on, this disciple took her into his home (John 19:26-27 NKJV).*

As Jesus hung there, He saw each one of us and was willing to suffer a horrific death so we could all be in heaven with Him one day.

The cross, an instrument of torture, became an instrument of life and a symbol of everlasting love. Two bars—one reaching up to heaven, one reaching out to the world. Amazing grace.

88

Who Do You Say I Am?

He said to them, but who do you say I am?
(Matthew 16:15 NKJV)

This is the most important question you will ever answer: Who do you say Jesus is? Many people accept that He existed, that He was a Jew from Galilee, and that He lived during the first century. Many also accept that He was martyred on the cross, and that His teachings were radical and influential. They are ready to accept Him as a great moral teacher, but not as the Son of God. But He could not possibly be a great moral teacher if He is not who He says He is. He would either be, at best, a liar or, at worst, mentally deranged. Most issues have shades of gray, but not this one.

C.S. Lewis sums it up beautifully:

> I am trying here to prevent anyone saying the really foolish thing that people often say about Him: 'I'm ready to accept Jesus as a great moral teacher, but I don't accept His claim to be God.' That is the one thing we must not say. A man who was merely a man and said the sort of thing Jesus said would not be a great moral teacher. He would either be a lunatic – on a level with the man who says he is a poached egg – or else he would be the Devil of Hell. You must make your choice.

Either this man was, and is, the Son of God: or else a madman or something worse. You can shut Him up for a fool, you can spit at Him and kill Him as a demon; or you can fall at His feet and call Him Lord and God.

But let us not come with any patronizing nonsense about His being a great human teacher. He has not left that open to us. He did not intend to. [1]

I know which one I believe—Jesus is the Son of God. Which do you believe? Ponder on this long and hard before you reply—the answer you arrive at will literally mean life or death.

81

The Gift of Choice

*Today I have given you a choice between life and death, success
and disaster.
(Deuteronomy 30:15 ERV)
Choose life so that you and your descendants may live.
(Deuteronomy 30:19 NRSV)*

God could have made an army of robots who would serve Him, but instead He made children who would love Him freely. One of the greatest gifts He offers us is the gift of choice. Throughout the Bible, we see Him honoring the choices made by His children.

Adam and Eve were the first people to walk the earth. They were given the choice of eating the fruit of the tree of the knowledge of good and evil or obeying God. They chose to eat the fruit with disastrous consequences for both them and future mankind.

Abel and Cain were the sons of Adam. Abel chose to honor God with his offering. Cain chose to murder his brother in a fit of jealous rage.

Lot had the choice of the grassy plain or the city of Sodom. He chose Sodom and the world. Abraham chose the plain and God's will.

David chose to follow God and became *"a man after God's own heart"* (1 Samuel 13:14 NKJV). Saul followed his own plan and ended up taking his own life on the battlefield.

On the day of Christ's crucifixion, two thieves hung on either side of Him. Once turned to Him for mercy; the other did not.

> *Then he said to Jesus, "Lord, remember me when You come into Your kingdom" (Luke 23:42 NKJV).*

Peter and Judas both denied their Lord. Peter wept bitterly and repented. Jesus returned for him and gave him mercy. On the day of His resurrection, an angel appeared to Mary Magdalene outside the tomb and told her to go tell His disciples that He was alive. But one disciple was especially called out—Peter.

> *But go, tell His disciples – AND PETER – that He is going before you into Galilee; there you will see Him, as He said to you (Mark 16:7 NKJV; emphasis mine).*

Judas opted to betray His master and, in the end, found death.

People often ask how a God of love can send people to hell. He doesn't. He simply honors their choice. He has provided each of us the way to Him. It is up to us to take it or leave it. This is the essence of free will.

> *Jesus answered, "I am the way and the truth and the life. No one comes to the Father except through me" (John 14:6 NKJV).*

God's gift—choice. Choose wisely.

Accepting Christ as Your Lord and Savior

*That if you confess with your mouth the Lord Jesus
and believe in your heart that God has raised Him from the dead, you
will be saved.*
(Romans 10:9 NKJV)

The greatest gift God has for you is eternal life, which He gives to those who come to Him through faith in His Son, Jesus Christ. If you truly believe Jesus is the Son of God, that He died on the Cross for your sins, that He was resurrected, and you want to accept Him as your Lord and Savior, you can do so by praying and asking Him into your life.

Below is a prayer which can be used as a guideline. If you want to use your own words, go ahead. He sees your heart; fancy words and phrases are not needed.

Lord,

I come to you just as I am, a sinner in need of a Savior. I believe you are the Son of God, that you died on the cross for me, that you rose on the third day and that you are now seated at the right hand of God the Father. I accept you as my Lord and Savior.

Thank you in Jesus' Name. Amen.

Notes

Acknowledgements

1. Unveiled Live, https://www.liveunveiled.com/.

3. The Heavens Declare the Glory of God

1. Amber Jorgensen, "NASA Images the Most Distant Galaxy Ever Resolved," Astronomy Magazine, http://www.astronomy.com/news/2018/01/nasa-images-the-most-distant-galaxy-ever-resolved.

2. Rob Garner, "Messier 51 (The Whirlpool Galaxy)," NASA, https://www.nasa.gov/feature/goddard/2017/messier-51-the-whirlpool-galaxy.

4. Fearfully and Wonderfully Made

1. Louis Giglio, *How Great is Our God DVD*, 2012, Sixstepsrecords.

2. The Franklin Institute, "Blood Vessels," https://www.fi.edu/heart/blood-vessels.

3. Piedmont Healthcare, "10 Fun Facts About Your Brain," https://www.piedmont.org/living-better/10-fun-facts-about-your-brain.

4. Brightside, "40 Incredible Facts About Your Eyes That You Never Imagined Were True," https://brightside.me/article/40-incredible-facts-about-your-eyes-which-you-never-imagined-were-true-24555/.

5. Rose Eveleth, Smithsonian Magazine, "There are 37.2 Trillion Cells in Your Body," https://www.smithsonianmag.com/smart-news/there-are-372-trillion-cells-in-your-body-4941473/.

6. C.S. Lewis, *The Problem of Pain* (NY: Harper Collins, 2001), 94.

6. Don't Avoid the Garden

1.   George Matheson, *Thoughts for Life's Journey* (A.C Armstrong, 1908), 266.

2.   Alexander Solzhenitsyn, *The Gulag Archipelago*, quoted in *Where is God When It Hurts,* Philip Yancey (Grand Rapids: Zondervan, 1990), 87.

8. Be Real

1. Charles Swindoll, *Growing Strong in the Seasons of Life* (Portland: Multnomah Press, 1983), 150.

2. National Geographic Website, "Blue Whale," https://www.nationalgeographic.com/animals/mammals/b/blue-whale/.

10. The Christian Country Club

1.   Max Lucado, *Outlive Your Life* (Nashville: Thomas Nelson, 2010), 24.

2.   A.W. Tozer, *The Pursuit of God* (Abbotsford: Aneko Press, 2015), 7.

16. Doubt vs. Unbelief

1.   Tim Keller, *Reason for God* (NY: Penguin Books, 2016), xvii.

21. No Scars?

1.   Matthew West, *The Healing Has Begun*, track 11, The *Story of Your Life,* 2018.

22. Every Tear is Precious

1.   Judith Orloff, MD, "The Healing Power of Tears," https://drjudithorloff.com/the-healing-power-of-tears/.

23. It is Well with My Soul

1.   Wikipedia, accessed July 1, 2019, https://en.wikipedia.org/wiki/Horatio_Spafford.

25. When You are Out of Oomph

1.   Andrew Peterson, *Always Good*, track 4, *Resurrection Letters,* 2018.

32. Lazarus

1.   John MacArthur, *The MacArthur New Testament Commentary, John 1-11* (Chicago: Moody Publishers, 2006). 461-462.

33. Stir Up Your Gift

1.   Louis Giglio, *How Great is Our God DVD*, 2012, Sixstepsrecords.

34. In the Crucible

1.   Crucible - a container of metal or refractory material employed for heating substances to heighten temperatures; a severe, searching test or trial. Dictionary.com, "crucible", accessed July 2, 2019 , https://www.dictionary.com/browse/crucible.

39. Age Is No Impediment

1.   Warren Wiersbe, *Be Basic, Genesis 1-11* (Colorado Springs: David C. Cook, 1998), 31.

46. In the Pit

1.   Joseph Bayly, *The View from a Hearse*, quoted in *Walking with God Through Pain and Suffering* - Tim Keller (NY: Penguin Books, 2010), 245

2.   Tim Keller, *Walking with God Through Pain and Suffering* (NY: Penguin Books, 2010), 243.

47. Dear "Younger Me"

1.   Mercy Me, *Dear Younger Me*, track 12, *I Can Only Imagine*, 2018.

50. The Fifth Sparrow

1.   Max Lucado, *Fearless* (Nashville: Thomas Nelson, 2009), 23.

2.   Dictionary.com, "masterpiece", accessed July 2, 2019 , https://www.dictionary.com/browse/masterpiece.

53. Betrayal

1. Tony Evans, *Detours* (Nashville: B&H Publishing Group, 2017).

58. Attrition of the Soul

1. C.S. Lewis, *The Screwtape Letters* (NY: Harper Collins, 2001), 155.

61. The Heart of the Father

1. Lee Strobel, *The Case for Grace* (Grand Rapids: Zondervan, 2015) 40.

2. Max Lucado, *Before Amen* (Nashville: Thomas Nelson, 2014), 11-12.

64. The Walls Will Fall

1. Max Lucado, *Glory Days* (Nashville: Thomas Nelson, 2015), 8.

74. Plant and Water

1. Mary Chapin Carpenter, *The Bug*, track 5, *Come On Come On,* 1992.

75. Words Need Action

1. Rebecca Manley Pippert, *Out of the Saltshaker and Into the World,* (Illinois: Intervarsity Press, 1999) 28, 98.

76. If You Ever Doubt His Love

1. Charles R. Swindoll, *Jesus* (Nashville: Thomas Nelson, 2008), 209.

80. Who Do You Say I Am?

1. C.S. Lewis, *Mere Christianity* (NY: Harper Collins, 2001), 52.

CPSIA information can be obtained
at www.ICGtesting.com
Printed in the USA
BVHW031631200819
556218BV00027B/109/P